T0272639

TEN INDIAN CLASSICS

TEN INDIAN CLASSICS

Foreword by
RANJIT HOSKOTE

MURTY CLASSICAL LIBRARY OF INDIA
HARVARD UNIVERSITY PRESS
Cambridge, Massachusetts
London, England
2025

SERIES DESIGN BY M9DESIGN

Library of Congress Cataloging-in-Publication Data

Names: Hoskote, Ranjit, 1969- writer of foreword.
Title: Ten Indian classics / foreword by Ranjit Hoskote.
Other titles: Murty classical library of India.
Description: Cambridge, Massachusetts :
Harvard University Press, 2025. |
Series: Murty classical library of India
Identifiers: LCCN 2024026579 | ISBN 9780674297142 (cloth) |
ISBN 9780674298224 (pdf) | ISBN 9780674298231 (epub)
Subjects: LCSH: Indic poetry—Early works to 1800—Translations into
English. | Epic poetry, Indic—Early works to 1800—Translations into
English. | Indic literature—Early works to 1800—Translations into
English. | Indic literature—Early works to 1800—Literary collections.
Classification: LCC PK2978.E5 T45 2025 |
DDC 891/.1—dc23/eng/20240802
LC record available at https://lccn.loc.gov/2024026579

CONTENTS

FOREWORD

Ranjit Hoskote

I

Published to celebrate the tenth anniversary of the Murty Classical Library of India, this anthology brings together a selection of ten moving and memorable extracts from the books that have appeared under the aegis of this series so far. These literary texts, written in South Asia across a period of 2,500 years, represent eight languages historically used in the subcontinent for scriptural and worldly purposes, for the composition of epic and hymn, poetry and satire, play and rhapsody, biography and visionary utterance. As I write "eight," a voice in my head corrects me: nine. This is fair, since the two extracts that represent Hindi here are drawn, respectively, from Braj Bhasha and Awadhi, robust and continuingly vibrant languages that are ancestral to the modern standard Hindi framed by academics and bureaucrats during the early twentieth century. Significantly, not one of the languages that appear in the pages of this anthology is dead. Even the seemingly remote classical languages of court, scriptorium, and monastic retreat—Sanskrit, Pali, and Persian—continue to exert their claims over the imagination of large numbers of readers, are read and resonate through the more everyday languages of South Asia and the South Asian global diaspora.

The Murty Classical Library of India (MCLI) is a courageous editorial enterprise that emerged from an auspicious conjunction of factors: a generous endowment made by the technological entrepreneur and friend of the humanities, Rohan Narayana Murty; the vision for such a series, developed by the distinguished Sanskritist and intellectual historian of South Asia, Sheldon Pollock, who served as the founding general editor to the series; and the stalwart commitment of Sharmila Sen, the editorial director of Harvard University Press, who gave this vision practical and perennial shape. The MCLI's mission, succinctly phrased on its website, is to "present the greatest literary works of India from the past two millennia to the largest readership in the world."

This has been achieved by a constellation of translators, editors, and designers whose devoted contributions have ensured a high degree of accomplishment in scholarship, literary quality, and design. It is the work of these contributors that breathes life into the distinctive MCLI facing-page editions, which carry both the Indic texts in their original script and their translations into English; the Indic scripts are presented in exquisite, specially commissioned typefaces, which have then been made available free of cost to other users to download for nonprofit use. The MCLI forms an invaluable addition to the other series dedicated to perennial literature that Harvard University Press publishes: the Loeb Classical Library, the Dumbarton Oaks Medieval Library, and the I Tatti Renaissance Library.

II

We zigzag across wide geographical expanses and journey from the sixth century B.C.E. to the nineteenth century C.E. as we traverse the extracts gathered in this anthology, beginning with the *Therīgāthā*, the songs of the earliest women to enter the Buddha's community of renunciates as nuns, translated from Pali by Charles Hallisey. These songs celebrate the transition from worldly life to spiritual renunciation and, compressed as they are, convey the richly detailed experience of the female questor. As the translator observes, the songs anthologized in the *Therīgāthā* may originally have been composed in a variety of ancient India's vernaculars and later rendered by editors into Pali, the lingua franca of early Buddhism; so that the present English translation takes its place in a genealogy of prior translations.

Bharavi's *Arjuna and the Hunter* (*Kirātārjunīya*), rendered from Sanskrit by Indira Viswanathan Peterson, is a court epic poem in eighteen chapters. It is the first court epic to have been composed around a single episode from the Mahabharata, a confrontation between the Pandava hero Arjuna and a hunter who turns out to be the supreme deity Shiva in disguise. It is also the first full-scale literary treatment of this episode, which would later become a popular literary subject in south India. The *Kirātārjunīya* is Bharavi's only known work; his dates are uncertain, with scholars placing him somewhere between the fourth and seventh centuries C.E..

Composed in the thirteenth century C.E., Raghavanka's *The Life of Harishchandra* (*Hariścandra Cāritra*) is regarded as a foundational poem in Kannada literature. It tells of a legendary king who refuses to abandon his duty to truth despite suffering horrific consequences. Raghavanka chose narrative materials from the Vedas and Puranas, radically transmuting them to create an ideal protagonist. As translator Vanamala Vishwanatha points out, the poet evolved a prosody aligned with contemporary speech patterns, which lent itself to song. Not surprisingly, the influence of Ragha-vanka's hero was felt well into the twentieth century, through the popular media of theater and cinema.

Allasani Peddana's *The Story of Manu* (*Manucaritramu*) embodies the political self-confidence and cultural magnif-icence of the sixteenth-century Vijayanagara empire. Trans-lated from Telugu by Velcheru Narayana Rao and David Shulman, it marks the breakthrough moment when, for the first time, a Telugu poet fused "a rather modern realism" with an "interest in the fantastic and the magical," in his translators' words, to produce a work of sumptuously ex-pressive artistry. Peddana's patron was the celebrated em-peror Krishnadevaraya; aptly, his account of Manu, the divinely descended ruler of myth, meditates both on the formation of human sensibility and on the responsibilities of kingship.

Guru Nanak's hymns emerge from Panjab's confluential culture, its religious imagination nourished by "Bhagats and Sufis, lovers of god from various Indic and Islamic tra-ditions," as translator Nikky-Guninder Kaur Singh phrases it. Across the late fifteenth and early sixteenth centuries C.E., the founder of the Sikh religion composed nearly a thousand hymns in Panjabi, collected into the Guru Granth Sahib, the core scripture of his followers, which includes the compositions of his successors as well as other mystics and teachers. Guru Nanak's Panjabi demonstrates a dazzling plurality, drawing on Siraiki and Khari Boli as well as San-skrit, Persian, and Arabic.

John Stratton Hawley's translation of *Sur's Ocean* (*Sūr-sāgar*) from Braj Bhasha brings this collection of poems attributed to a sixteenth-century devotional poet into circulation for a present-day Anglophone audience. "Surdas" more accurately describes a literary tradition than an individual: the earliest dated *Sūrsāgar* manuscript, containing 239 poems attributed to Surdas, was written in 1582; by the nineteenth century, it had swelled to properly oceanic proportions with nearly ten thousand poems. While the god Krishna is its protagonist, the *Sūrsāgar* blurs the line between sensuousness and spirituality, court and temple. This is consonant with Braj Bhasha literature's focus on love's delights and vicissitudes.

Tulsidas was a contemporary of two of the most influential Mughal emperors, Akbar and Jahangir, both of whom commissioned numerous translations of Hindu epics and philosophical texts from Sanskrit into Persian. A votary of the god-king Ram, Tulsidas is best known for his *The Epic of Ram* (*Rāmcaritmānas* literally, "Divine Lake of Ram's Deeds"), translated here by Philip Lutgendorf. Composed in Awadhi in 1574 C.E., the *The Epic of Ram* was disseminated by wandering singers, reciters, and scholars; it soon received widespread veneration. By the twentieth century, it was enshrined both in the nascent Hindi literary canon and in the popular imagination.

Wheeler M. Thackston takes us deep into the extraordinary life and turbulent times of the third Mughal emperor through his translation of the scholar-courtier Abu'l-Fazl's *The History of Akbar* (*Akbarnāma*) from Persian. No mere chronicle, it legitimized the emperor's ideology of divine kingship: it presented Akbar as the perfect embodiment of a mystical light inherited, through both Genghis Khan and Taimur Lang (Tamerlane, in European records), from a remote Central Asian ancestress. The panegyric was still in process when its author was assassinated in 1602 C.E. on the orders of Akbar's son, the future emperor Jahangir, then in revolt against his father.

Christopher Shackle brings over for us, from Panjabi, the poetry of the eighteenth-century mystic Bullhe Shah, who is venerated on both sides of the India-Pakistan border as the most majestic among Panjab's Sufis. The power of love to harmonize all beings into a cosmic unity is Bullhe Shah's leitmotif; the emotional appeal of his passionate songs of surrender before the Divine carries across national, religious, ethnic, and generational lines. Bullhe Shah is as likely to be read on the page today as he is to be heard at popular music concerts, on stage, and on television and the big screen.

The tenth extract presented here comprises a suite of poems by the magisterial Mir Taqi Mir (1723–1810), translated from Urdu by Shamsur Rahman Faruqi, who, alas, is no longer with us. Faruqi-saab, as he was known to his admirers, was immersed in Mir's *divan,* its testimony to love, doubt, irony, torment, and the fear of mortality crafted even as the Mughal empire collapsed under the combined, rapacious pressure of invaders from the northwest and the British East India Company. Serially displaced from cities he regarded as home, his lifeworld in ruins, Mir belongs strikingly to our own vexed, precarious times.

We trust that this selection of translations will persuade

many readers to make their way to the facing-page editions from which they have been chosen, to savor the bridging of the distance between one language and another, one script and another. The labor of editors often goes unremarked in such projects; it disappears elegantly and seamlessly into the fabric as finally woven. To the MCLI editors who worked closely with translators, offering responses and suggestions, sharing their knowledge and insights in a spirit of collegiality, we offer our admiration and gratitude: Sheldon Pollock, David Shulman, Monika Horstmann, Sunil Sharma, Francesca Orsini, and Archana Venkatesan.

III

While this anthology features eight—or, as the voice in my head insists, nine—of South Asia's languages, it invites the reader to engage with the region in its multilingual plenitude, its many literatures. Some measure of South Asia's linguistic diversity may be gauged from the fact that India's constitution recognizes twenty-two languages as "scheduled languages"; meanwhile, according to the 2001 Census of India, there are 122 "major" languages and 1,599 "other" languages in use across the country. Of these, thirty languages are spoken by more than a million people each. Many of these languages are spoken not only in India but also across the comparatively recent territorial borders that demarcate South Asia into nation-states, in Pakistan, Afghanistan, Bangladesh, Nepal, Bhutan, Sri Lanka, and the Maldives.

Importantly, each of South Asia's literatures is closely connected to a living tradition, which spans varied media and mutates with shifts in regional and sectarian context.

These living traditions are constantly being reframed by various cultural agents, through the lenses of aesthetics and ideology, into public outcomes that far exceed the scholarly boundaries of the annotated critical edition. South Asia's literary classics must therefore be seen as texts continually caught up in a lively interplay with many other forms of cultural expression available through oral narrative, scribal record, performance, and print, as well as ranging across the classical, folk, and mediatic domains of experience. These would include scripture, recitation or storytelling, dance or theater, ritual ceremonies, as well as cinema, television, and comics.

Indeed, it could be argued that classical texts become widely available in South Asia *precisely* through such an interplay, rather than through the sovereign authority of the book. This insight lies at the heart of the assertion famously attributed—invariably in some misquoted or mangled form —to the renowned poet, translator, and cultural anthropologist A. K. Ramanujan: "No Indian reads the Ramayana [or the Mahabharata, the epics are switched at will, depending on who's passing on the story] for the first time."[1]

To set the record straight, this is what Ramanujan actually wrote:

"No Hindu ever reads the *Mahābhārata* for the first time. And when he does get to read it, he doesn't usually read it in Sanskrit. As one such native, I know the Hindu epics, not as a Sanskritist (which I am not), but through Kannada and Tamil, mostly through the oral traditions.

I've heard bits and pieces of it in a tailor's shop where a pundit used to regale us with *Mahābhārata* stories and large sections of a sixteenth-century Kannada text; from brahman cooks in the house; from an older boy who loved to keep us spellbound with it ... in the evenings, under a large *neem* tree in a wealthy engineer's compound; from a somewhat bored algebra teacher who switched from the binomial theorem to the problems of Draupadi and her five husbands. Then there were professional bards [who] would recite, sing and tell the *Mahābhārata* in sections night after night.... They sang songs in several languages, told folktales, sometimes danced, quoted Sanskrit tags as well as the daily newspaper, and made the *Mahābhārata* entertaining, didactic and relevant to the listener's present."[2]

Ramanujan situates this relay of South Asia's classical narratives across vernacular genres in the public sphere, their intuitive rather than schooled transmission through home culture, and their dissemination through popular media in a broadly Hindu milieu. It should be clarified that the same processes have also long been integral to the cultural experience of many Indians belonging to other religious groups. Elsewhere, he discusses the historical circulation of the other major Indian epic, the Ramayana, across South and Southeast Asia through a bewildering array of narrative, discursive, and performative forms, with Ram transformed variously into a Bodhisattva by Theravada monks and into an Islamic hero by the puppet masters of the wayang shadow theater. This leads him to dispense entirely with the notion of a single true and pure original of the epic: "I have come to prefer the word *tellings* to the usual terms *versions* or *variants* because the latter terms can and typically do imply that there is an invariant, an original or *Ur*-text—usually Valmiki's Sanskrit *Rāmāyana,* the earliest and most prestigious of them all. But as we shall see, it is not always Valmiki's narrative that is carried from one language to another."[3]

With their picaresque, playfully unreliable narrators and their riffing, improvisatory energies, these rather colorful scenarios of the transmission of the Indian classics appear to be quite unlike that of the Greek and Latin classics, which are no longer linked to a collective living tradition. True, at one level, they are regarded with reverence as providing "Western" culture with its enlightened civilizational basis. And yet, on looking closely, one might be forgiven for noticing that women and slaves could not vote under the rules of Athenian democracy, while Roman political choices tended more toward authoritarian templates of empire than liberal models for a republic. Undeniably, too, the Greek and Latin classics manifest themselves consistently through a Warburgian *Nachleben der Antike,* an "afterlife of the classical," in the visual arts, literature, theater, and cinema. Hardly a year goes by, for instance, without a novelist invoking the shades of the Odyssey, a contemporary poet translating or critically adapting Ovid's *Metamorphoses,* and the Argonauts being incarnated in futuristic avatars on the screen. For the most part, though—and particularly through a lineage of scholarship that goes back to the Renaissance humanists—these classics of the ancient Aegean and Mediterranean worlds have been domesticated and reconstituted as relevant to elite academic and literary discourse rather than to the lived experience of rituals, seasonal ceremonials, and festivals articulated across social classes.

IV

So far, this foreword has focused on the South Asian cultural world as seen from within. We come now to the next, and vital, question: How have translators carried these seemingly culture-specific texts beyond the interiority of "being Indian," when all they have had to work with are the conventions and strategies of a target language, unattended by the multilayered, multidimensional ethos of the source languages? And crucially, while we see that these classics might bear significance for the more-or-less direct heirs of the people for whom they were originally written, why should they matter to those who have no direct genealogical or regional connection with the context of composition?

There is a key historical circumstance to be considered here. We approach the South Asian classics, inevitably, in a postcolonial spirit, in full awareness of the asymmetries and injustices, the missed opportunities for mutual understanding, and the lingering, deliberate estrangement from the insistently familiar that characterized the colonial encounter. The practice of translation, in such a situation, is conditioned by debates around Orientalism and decolonization, and by the interpretive paradigms of Indology, comparative literature, comparative religion, and cultural anthropology.

The situation is fertile in ironies and occupational hazards. Non-Indians working with Indian materials cross the limen from outside to inside, however provisionally, shuttling between an observer's impossible neutrality and a participant's infectious enthusiasm. Indians working with what might be regarded as their "own" materials might wish for more distance from it, or ask themselves whether Indians trained in Indology are really just a subcaste of the Orientalist community. An empathetic yet critical knowledge is the only touchstone of *adhikāra,* or authoritative competence, here, not a flat nativist claim to cultural authenticity or an insistence on the primacy of dry textual exegesis.

These existential questions have very practical implications. When translating South Asia's classics, how do we regard such texts? As riddling philological puzzles or as exotic cultural curiosities? Or as literary provocations to wrestle with, in the conviction that they will have something to say to us about our own lives and dreams, affections and beliefs, struggles with faith, negotiations with doubt; our thresholds of hope and despair, love and anguish?

Any translation that is made today from South Asia's literatures—whether classical or contemporary—must be made in full awareness of the region's fraught ideological conflicts and their impact on its languages. Sanskrit in India and Urdu in Pakistan, for instance, have been pressed into service as symbols of a dominant culture. Narrowed to fit such a role, Sanskrit becomes overidentified with pious scriptural texts, to the exclusion of its sensuous, worldly literary treasures. Likewise, Urdu becomes synonymous with an elevated Perso-Arabic register, eclipsing its origins in an earthy, eclectic Hindavi usage quickened by Braj Bhasha and Khari Boli. Meanwhile, the postcolonial nation-state inherits, from the modern European template of nationhood, an ideological obsession with a single, unifying national language. Consequently, its attempts at imposing one official language on a historically polyglot society result in a tension between the center and the regions.

Ironically, the same principle of associating every nation with a single language plays out at the regional level too, with socially or culturally dominant local groups imposing their tongue on other groups, whose own tongues are demoted to the status of "dialects"—thus illustrating the sociolinguist Max Weinrich's wry observation that "a language is a dialect with an army and a navy."[4] In the northwest, for instance, Panjabi has marginalized Siraiki. Across the Gangetic belt, modern Hindi has subjugated a spectrum of languages including Kannauji, Magahi, Bhojpuri, Bundeli, Bagheli, and Chhattisgarhi. And while many of South Asia's regional languages have established a global reach through the diaspora, they remain vulnerable at home due to a lack of institutional support and an erosion of readership, due partly to the spread of influential link languages like English and Hindi, and partly to the ascendancy of the electronic media.

Operating in such a complex palimpsestic terrain, then, the finest translators of South Asian texts have been impelled by a generous intellectual curiosity, a sense of solidarity with vulnerable literatures and their embattled guardians, or the desire to enrich and expand their artistic sensibility through dialogue with a cultural other—in each case, by a hermeneutics of surprise.

V

All the translations that appear in this anthology are informed by the same fundamental question: How do we find the optimal language into which to render these texts? By which I do not mean a satisfactory set of solutions within the parameters of an admittedly absorbent and flexible English, but rather, a subtle architecture of nuance, register, tonality, familiarity, and strangeness that forms a third linguistic space beyond the binary of source and target language. A space that offers us revolving routes of discovery, difficulty and epiphany; that offers us gateways to forms of thought, imagination, and being that we may never have chanced upon before. I pause to think back to an extraordinary essay that the anthropologist Clifford Geertz published in 1977 on the possibility—and the perils—of entering a space of encounter with other societies or periods and their cultural productions. This essay was presented as an act of homage to the literary critic Lionel Trilling; toward its conclusion, Geertz suggested that, both for Trilling and himself, one of the "significant mysteries" of humankind's cultural life involved addressing "how it is that other people's creations can be so utterly their own and so deeply part of us."[5]

As a rider to this inspiring and potentially transformative mystery, I would add the last, most defiant of the fourteen working definitions of a classic that the Italian novelist and essayist Italo Calvino offered in a compelling 1981 essay: "A classic is a work which persists as background noise even when a present that is totally incompatible with it holds sway."[6]

This, perhaps, is all the justification we need when asked the usual questions: What are the classics for? In what does their perennial and universal value reside? Why do we return to the classics? How do they replenish, excite, or console us? And why do we share them?

What the classics that transit across the world's borders in translation really do is invite us to step outside our zones of cultural comfort. They suggest that we could learn to appreciate the contours of thought and imagination from elsewhere and elsewhen. They educate us in an actively cosmopolitan sensibility, as a community of readers unconstrained by narrow definitions of identity and belonging, as participants in a *Weltliteratur* that does not subordinate the world's literatures to a dominant model but builds into a polyphonic, kaleidoscopic assembly of them all.

What you hold in your hands, dear reader, are not the residues of vanished civilizations disturbed from their eternal rest in the archive of lost times. We hope that these poems and stories will resonate for you, find a place in your hearts, as prompts both to the visceral excitement and the generative disorientation of discovery.

1.

Selections from the
Therīgāthā

by the First Buddhist Women

*Translated from Pali
by Charles Hallisey*

⸺

The *Therīgāthā* is an anthology of poems by and about the first Buddhist women. These women were *therīs*, "senior ones," among ordained Buddhist women, and they bore that epithet because of their religious achievements. The *therīs* are enlightened women and most of the poems (*gāthā*) in the anthology are songs about their experiences. Dhammapala, the sixth-century Buddhist commentator on the *Therīgāthā*, calls the *therīs'* poems *udāna*, "inspired utterances," and by doing so, he associated the work with a venerable Buddhist speech genre. For Dhammapala, the characteristic mark of "the utterance" would be "one or more verses consisting of knowledge about some situation accompanied by the euphoria that is felt there, for an *udāna* is proclaimed by way of a composition of verses and caused to rise up through joy and euphoria."[1]

Individual poems in the *Therīgāthā* were composed over a considerable period, perhaps centuries; according to Buddhist tradition, they date from the time of the Buddha himself, while according to modern historical methods, some date as late as the end of the third century B.C.E.[2]

The poems as we receive them are in Pali, the scholarly and religious language distinctive to the Theravadin Buddhist traditions that are now found in Sri Lanka and Southeast Asia; in the first millennium, however, Theravada Buddhism was quite prominent in south India as well. It seems likely that these verses have been "translated" from whatever their original versions may have been in any number of ancient Indian vernaculars and then reworked as Pali evolved. The "translation" of the poems in the *Therīgāthā* into Pali was key to their wide circulation.

Basic ideas common to all schools of early Buddhism are clear in the *Therīgāthā*. These include ideas about the nature of the world that early Buddhism shared with other Indian religions, such as the ideas of rebirth and karma that structure the conditions of experience and action for beings as they are reborn in samsara. Early Buddhism affirmed that a complete liberation from samsara was possible. This liberation is nirvana, or nibbana, and many of the *udānas* of the first Buddhist women express the joy of the *therīs* at the achievement of this state.

Ideas distinctive to early Indian Buddhism are also obvious. These include the Four Noble Truths that the Buddha taught in his first sermon, "Setting in Motion the Wheel of Truth": all this is suffering; suffering has a cause; suffering can be ended; and there is a path to that end, the noble eightfold path.[3]

In general, the poems of the *Therīgāthā* wear their Buddhist doctrine quite lightly, and they avoid most specifics of Buddhist practice. They celebrate individual transformation that ends in liberation and also display a moral acuity and keen perception of social realities that are less visible in most other early Buddhist texts.

These poems are composed by some of the *first* Buddhists; they are some of the *first* poetry of India; they are some of the *first* by women in India; this is the *first* collection of women's literature in the world. However, the *Therīgāthā* is more than a collection of historical evidence of the needs, aspirations, and achievements of some of the first Buddhist women. Its poems enable us to see things that we have not seen before and to imagine things that we have not dreamed before. They give us a chance to be free from ourselves and from our ususal places in the world—at least imaginatively— and to glimpse a different potential for ourselves. The poems in the *Therīgāthā* are *udānas* about the joy of being free, and they hold out the promise, in the pleasure that they give, of being the occasion for making us free, too.

POEMS WITH ONE VERSE

Therika

Spoken by the Buddha to her

Now that you live among *therīs*, Therika,[4]
the name you were given as a child finally becomes you.

So sleep well, covered with cloth you have made,
your passion for sex shriveled away
like a herb dried up in a pot.

3

Mutta

Spoken by the Buddha to her

The name you are called by means freed, Mutta,[5]

so be freed from what holds you back,
like the moon from the grasp of Rahu[6]
at the end of an eclipse.
When nothing is owed because the mind is completely free
you can relish food collected as alms.

Punna

Spoken by the Buddha to her

The name you are called by means full, Punna,[7]

so be filled with good things, like the moon when it is full,
break through all that is dark with wisdom made full.

Tissa

Spoken by the Buddha to her

Tissa, train yourself strictly, don't let
what can hold you back overwhelm you.[8]
When you are free from everything that holds you back
you can live in the world
without the depravities that ooze out from within.

Another Tissa

Addressing herself, repeating what was spoken by the Buddha to her

Tissa, hold fast to good things, don't let the moment
    escape.[9]
Those who end up in hell cry over moments now past.

Dhira

Addressing herself, repeating what was spoken by the Buddha to her

The name you are called by means self-reliance, Dhira,

so know these for yourself:
cessation, the stilling of projections, happiness.
Attain nibbana, unsurpassed safety from all that holds you
    back.

Vira

Addressing herself, repeating what was spoken by the Buddha to her

The name you are called by means hero, Vira,

it's a good name for you because of your heroic qualities,
you are a nun who knows how to know well.[10]
Take care of the body, it's your last,
just make sure it doesn't become a vehicle for death after
    this.

Mitta

Addressing herself, repeating what was spoken by the Buddha to her

The name you are called by means friend, Mitta,

you became a nun out of faith,
now be someone who delights in friends,
become morally skillful
for the sake of that unsurpassed safety from all that holds
    you back.

Bhadra

Addressing herself, repeating what was spoken by the Buddha to her

The name you are called by means auspicious, Bhadra,

you became a nun out of faith,
now be someone who delights in auspicious things,
become morally skillful
for the sake of that unsurpassed safety from all that holds
    you back.

Upasama

Addressing herself, repeating what was spoken by the Buddha to her

The name you are called by means calm, Upasama,

you should cross the flood where death holds sway,
hard as it is to cross.

Take care of the body, it's your last,
but make sure it doesn't become a vehicle for death after
    this.

Mutta

The name I am called by means freed

and I am quite free, well-free from three crooked things,
mortar, pestle, and husband with his own crooked thing.[11]
I am freed from birth and death,
what leads to rebirth has been rooted out.

Dhammadinna

She who has given rise to the wish for freedom
and is set on it, shall be clear in mind.[12]
One whose heart is not caught in the pleasures of the
    senses,
one who is bound upstream, will be freed.[13]

Visakha

Do what the Buddha taught,
there's nothing to be sorry about after doing it.[14]
Quick, wash the feet, sit down off to one side.

Sumana

Once you see as suffering[15]
even the basic bits that make up everything,[16]
you won't be born again,
calm is how you will live
once you discard the desire for more lives.

Uttara

Self-controlled with the body,
with speech, and with the mind,
having pulled out craving down to the root,
I have become cool, free.[17]

Sumana who renounced in old age
Addressing herself

Sleep well, dear old one,
covered with cloth you have made,
your passion for sex has shriveled away,
you've become cool, free.[18]

Dhamma

Wandering about for alms,
but weak, leaning on a stick with limbs shaking,

I fell to the ground right there,
and seeing the danger in the body, my heart was freed.[19]

Sangha

Abandoning houses, going forth,
giving up son, livestock, and all that is dear,
leaving behind desire, anger, and ignorance,
discarding them all,
having pulled out craving down to the root,
I have become cool, I am free.[20]

THE GREAT CHAPTER

Sumedha

When I was Sumedha,[21]
the daughter of King Konca of Mantavati and his chief
    queen,
I was converted by those who live what the Buddha
    taught.[22]

Through them, I became virtuous, eloquent, learned,
disciplined in the teaching of the Buddha,
and I came to my parents and said,
"May you both listen carefully.

9

"I delight in nibbana,
everything about life is uncertain
even if it is the life of a god,
why would I delight in things not worth desiring,
things with so little pleasure and so much annoyance.

"Everything that the senses desire is bitter,
but fools swoon over such poisonous things
only to end up in hell for a long time,
there they suffer and in the end they are destroyed.

"Such fools cannot control what they do
with their body, speech, or mind,
weeping wherever they are punished
for their own evil actions,
always increasing evil for themselves.

"They are fools, unwise, heedless,
locked up in their own suffering as it arises,
even when someone tries to teach them,
they are oblivious, not realizing
that they are living out the noble truths.[23]

"Mother, most people cannot understand
these truths taught by the Buddha,
they take pleasure in everything about life
and they long to be born among gods.

"Even birth among gods is uncertain,
it is only birth in another place just as impermanent,

but somehow fools are not terrified
of being born again and again.

"There are four places of punishment
and two other ones where we are somehow reborn.[24]
There is no going forth from hell
once you are there to be punished.[25]

"Give me permission, both of you, to go forth now
in the teaching of the Buddha, the one with ten powers,[26]
I do not have other responsibilities and I will exert myself
to make an end of birth and death.

"I am finished with delighting in just being alive,
I am finished too with the misfortune of having a body,
Give me permission and I will go forth
for the sake of ending the craving for existence.

"When Buddhas appear
bad luck can be avoided and good luck can be had;
for as long as I live, I will keep my moral precepts,
I will not defame the holy life."

Then Sumedha said to her mother and father,
"I will not eat any more food as a householder,
if I do not receive permission to go forth,[27]
I will be in your house, but I might as well be dead."

Her mother suffered and cried
and her father's face was covered with tears,

they tried to reason with Sumedha
who had fallen to the palace floor.

"Get up, child, what are these tears for?
You are already promised in marriage,
you have been given to handsome King Anikadatta
who is in Varanavati.

"You will be the wife of King Anikadatta,
his chief queen, and remember, child,
keeping moral precepts, living the holy life,
going forth, all that is hard to do.

"In kingship, there is authority, wealth, power,
things to enjoy and happiness.
You are a young girl, enjoy the pleasures of the body
and enjoy wealth. Let your wedding take place, child."

Sumedha answered them,
"It's not like that at all, existence is worthless,
I will either go forth or I will die,
but I won't get married.

"Why should I cling, like a worm,
to a body that will only turn into a corpse,
a sack always oozing, frightening, stinking
foul and putrid, filled with foul things?[28]

"I certainly know what the body is like.
It is repulsive, a corpse, food for birds and worms,

12

covered with flesh and blood,
so why is it to be given in marriage?

"This body will soon be carried,
without consciousness, to the cemetery,
it will be discarded like a log
by disgusted relatives.

"After they have thrown it away as food for others,
even one's own mother and father, disgusted, wash
    themselves,
and it has to be even more disgusting for everyone.

"People cling to this body,
even though it has no essence,
and is only a tangle of bones and sinews,
a foul body filled with spit, tears, feces, and urine.

"If one's own mother were to open it up
and pull what is inside of it outside,
even she would not be able to stand the stench
and would be disgusted by it.

"If I consider carefully what makes a person
the senses and their objects, the basic elements
that make up everything,[29] I see that all of it is
    constructed,

it is all rooted in birth and is the condition for suffering,
 so why would I want to get married?

"Even if three hundred new swords were to cut my body
day after day for a hundred years,
it would be worth it
if it brought an end to suffering.

"Anyone would put this carnage on themselves
once they understood the instruction of the teacher,
samsara is long for those
who are reborn again and again
only to be killed again and again.

"There is no end
to the carnage that occurs in samsara,
among gods and humans,
among animals, asuras, and hungry ghosts, and also in
        hells.[30]

"There is so much carnage
for those who are in hells for punishment,
but even for gods there is no safe place.
There is nothing better than the happiness of nibbana.

"Those who have reached nibbana
are the ones who are disciplined
by the teaching of the one with ten powers,[31]
living at ease, they strive to end birth and death.

"Today, Father, I will go renounce,
what good are insubstantial pleasures?

I am fed up with what pleases the senses,
all of it is like vomit,
like a palm-tree with its top cut off."[32]

While she was speaking in this way to her father,
Anikadatta, to whom she was promised in marriage,
arrived in the city of Varanavati at the time set for the
    wedding.[33]

Right at that moment, Sumedha cut her hair,
black, thick, and soft, with a knife,
she went inside the palace and closed herself inside it
and closed herself inside herself into the first *jhāna*.[34]

Anikadatta had reached the city
at the same time that she went into that happy state,
inside the palace, Sumedha developed
her perceptions of impermanence.

While she was focusing her attention in meditation,
Anikadatta entered the palace in a hurry,
his body even more beautiful with jewels and gold,
and he entreated Sumedha respectfully.

"In kingship, there is authority, wealth, power,
things to enjoy and happiness.
You are a young girl,
enjoy the pleasures of the body,[35]
happiness for the body is rare in this world.

"The kingdom is bestowed on you,[36]
enjoy what is meant to be enjoyed, and be generous,
do not be sad yourself, you are making your parents
    suffer."

But Sumedha knew that the urges of the senses lead
    nowhere
and her delusions about the world were gone.
She began to speak, "You should not delight
in the pleasures of the senses, look at the dangers in them.

 "Mandhata was a king of the known world,
no one had more wealth or pleasure than him,
but even he died unsatisfied,
his wants unfulfilled.[37]

"Even if it were to rain every kind of jewel,
enough to fill the ten directions,
still there would be no satisfying the desires of the senses.
Humans always die unsatisfied.

"The pleasures of the senses are like a slaughterhouse,
they are like a snake's head, they burn like a torch,
they give as much pleasure as a skeleton.

"The pleasures of the senses are impermanent
inconstant, they come with sufferings,
they are strong poisons, a hot iron ball down the throat,
they are the root of pain, and suffering is their fruit.

"The pleasures of the senses are like the fruits of a tree,[38]
like pieces of meat, pain is what they are,
the pleasures of the senses deceive like a dream,
they are like borrowed goods.

"The pleasures of the senses are like swords and stakes,
like disease, like an abscess, painful and hurtful,
they are like a pit of burning coals,
the root of pain, fearful and fatal.

"The pleasures of the senses bring many sufferings,
those who know call them hindrances,
you should go,
I myself don't trust existence.

"What can another do for me
when his own head is on fire?
When old age and death are right behind one,
one must try to end them."

At that point, Sumedha opened the door
and saw her mother and father, and also Anikadatta
all seated on the floor, crying,
and she said this to them:

"Samsara is long for fools
and for those who cry over and over
over the death of a father
or the killing of a brother or their own death.

"When you remember samsara
as it really is for beings,
remember the tears, the mothers' milk, the blood,
the mountain of bones of those born again and again.

"Think of the oceans when remembering the tears,
the mothers' milk, and the blood,
think of Mt. Vipula
when counting the bones that just one being has had.[39]

"If the whole continent of Jambudvipa
were broken up into little balls
the size of small fruits,
the number of them would still be less
than the number of mothers and grandmothers you have
        had.

"Think about all the grass, sticks, and leaves there are,
even if they were broken into smaller pieces
they would still be less than the fathers and grandfathers
        you have had.

"Remember the blind turtle in the eastern sea
and the hole in the yoke floating in another ocean,
remember how the turtle put his head through the yoke,
that is our chances of having a human birth.

"Remember the body, it has no essence inside,
a misfortune in itself, no more than a ball of foam,

look at what makes a person, it is all impermanent,
think of the hells filled with carnage.

"Remember all those who keep on filling cemeteries,
remember to fear becoming a 'crocodile,'
remember the four noble truths.[40]

"When you could taste sweet ambrosia,[41]
why would you want to taste the five bitter things?[42]
And the pleasures of the senses
are actually more bitter than the five bitter things.

"When the sweet ambrosia of the deathless exists,
why would you want the pleasures of the senses that are
        painful?
All the delights of the senses burn, are rotten,
troubled, and are seething.

"When friends exist,
why would you want the pleasures of the senses
that are only so many enemies?
They are like kings, thieves, floods, and disliked people
in how harmful they are to you.

"When freedom exists, why would anyone want
imprisonment and execution?
In the pleasures of the senses, people experience
the sufferings of bondage and beatings against their will.

"A bundle of grass, when set on fire,
burns the one who holds it and does not let go,
the pleasures of the senses are like torches
that will not let go of anyone who held them.

"Why abandon a big happiness
because of the little happiness that the urges of the senses
      promise?
Do not suffer later like the *puthuloma* fish
who swallows the hook just to eat the bait.

"When among those things that please the senses,
control what the senses urge, just as a dog is held by a
      chain,
otherwise the urges of the senses will kick you about
like a low-caste person does to a dog.

"If you get yoked to the pleasures of the senses,
you will experience no end of suffering,
so many sadnesses of the mind,
so give up such unreliable pleasures.

"When there can be no aging,
why would anyone want the pleasures of the senses,
since aging itself is in their midst,
just as sickness and death always come together with
      birth?

"This is something that has no old age, it has no death,
this is the sorrowless state,

without old age and death,
without enmity, without crowding,
without failure, without fear, without trouble.

"This state without death has been attained by many,
it should be attained today by us,
the one who applies himself easily can,
but it is not possible for one who does not strive."

As Sumedha spoke, she took no delight
in the constructed appearances of the world,[43]
but finally to convince Anikadatta,
she threw the hair she had cut off on the floor.

Anikadatta stood up and joined his hands respectfully,
he asked her father to allow Sumedha to go forth
so she could see nibbana and the four noble truths.

Allowed to go by her mother and father,
she went forth, frightened as she was by the sorrows that
    otherwise had to come,[44]
and she realized the six higher powers and the highest
    fruit
while she was still being trained.[45]

The attainment of nibbana for that king's daughter
was marvelous and unusual,
but equally so was what she said about her previous
    existences:

"When the Lord Buddha Konagamana was
in a new residence in a monastery,
I was one of three woman friends
who gave a *vihara* to him[46]

"As a result of that, we were born among gods
ten times, one hundred times,
one thousand times, ten thousand times,
who can say how many times
we were born among humans just from that gift.

"When we were born among gods, we had great powers,
and it was the same when we were born among humans,
I was even the chief queen, the gem of a woman,
for a king who was a lord of the whole world.

"That gift was the root cause for my sense of peace
in the teaching of the Buddha,
that first encounter with that previous Buddha
led to nibbana for me who delighted in his dhamma.

"Those who trust the teaching
of the one who has perfect wisdom
and do what he teaches,
they become disgusted with existence,
and turning away from it,
they set themselves free."

2.

Selections from
Arjuna and the Hunter

by Bharavi

Translated from Sanskrit
by Indira Viswanathan Peterson

Arjuna and the Hunter (*Kirātārjunīya*), the only known work by
Bharavi, is a Sanskrit court epic poem in eighteen chapters and 1,040
verses. It narrates the hero Arjuna's combat with the god Shiva in
the guise of a hunter, an important episode in the *Āraṇyakaparvan*
(Forest Book) of the Mahabharata, the epic of the great war of the
Kuru clans.[1] *Arjuna* is celebrated as one of the five masterpieces of
the court epic (*mahākāvya*) genre, the most prestigious genre of
classical Sanskrit poetry.[2]

As is the case with many early Sanskrit authors, very little is
known about Bharavi. He appears to have flourished in south In-
dia, sometime between the fourth and seventh century. Ravikirti,
a panegyrist of the Chalukya king Pulakeshin II, named Bharavi
and Kalidasa as famous poets in an inscription from 634 C.E.[3] Dan-
din, a generation after Ravikirti and author of *The Mirror for Poetry,*
a pioneering work on poetics, associated Bharavi with the Pallavas
and other south Indian kings.[4]

Bharavi was the first poet to write a court epic on a Mahabharata episode, and this is also the first full-fledged literary treatment of the narrative of the hero and the hunter, which became a popular theme in south Indian literature and art after the seventh century. With *Arjuna*, he established court epic as the premier arena for the dazzling displays of virtuosity that were to become the hallmark of poetic craft in Sanskrit. While Bharavi worked within a literary tradition that prized norm and convention, his poem bears the stamp of his distinctive voice and many innovations in form and style—such as the prominence of long, eloquent speeches—that then became the norm. He offers a greater variety of meters, longer chapters, and longer speeches and descriptions than earlier poets, all features that became entrenched in the court epic style.[5] *Arjuna* had become a seminal text in the Sanskrit literary canon almost from its origins, and remains so to this day.

Sanskrit *mahakavyas*—finely crafted poems written for learned readers that treat exalted heroes and elevated themes—have much in common with literary epics such as Virgil's *Aeneid*.[6] While not always based on older epic narratives, the typical *mahākāvya* traces the exploits of a noble hero, culminating in his victory over enemies or adverse forces.[7] They are also distinguished by extended treatment of aspects of political life and courtly culture, myth, legend, and landscape. Court epics are also required to treat "the fruits of the four aims of life," that is, to embrace the whole range of human aspiration, touching on the moral life, wealth and success, pleasure, and transcendence over karma and mundane existence.[8] Lastly, *mahākāvyas* are expected to evoke an overarching aesthetic emotion (*rasa*), resonating with fundamental, powerful human emotions, most prominently the heroic and the erotic.[9]

In the Mahabharata episode on which Bharavi based his poem, the Pandava hero Arjuna performs ascetic self-mortification (*tapas*) in a Himalayan forest in order to win Shiva's favor and obtain the boon of a supernatural weapon from him. The Pashupata weapon will help the five Pandava brothers to overcome their cousins, the Kauravas, in their just war and regain the kingdom that the Kauravas had taken in a rigged dicing match. The drama of *Arjuna and the Hunter* turns on the trial Shiva sets for the hero. Disguised as a *kirāta,* a hunter from a mountain tribe, Shiva picks a quarrel with Arjuna and tests his courage in combat, ultimately revealing himself and granting him the desired weapon. The epic narrative illuminates heroic action, sacred duty, and cosmo-moral order (dharma), self-restraint and austerity, devotion (bhakti) and divine benevolence—core values in the culture of ancient India's Brahman and warrior elites and enduring themes in the Hindu tradition. The choice of this episode enables Bharavi to plunge immediately and dramatically into ethical and political issues.

In this excerpt, the god Indra subjects Arjuna to yet another test. Arriving at Arjuna's hermitage disguised as an aged Brahman, he questions the appropriateness of a warrior undertaking austerity. Asceticism, Indra argues, should be performed solely by world renouncers, to attain liberation from existence. Arjuna fiercely defends his asceticism, saying that his guru has instructed him to please the warrior god Indra. Indra reveals his identity and directs Arjuna to propitiate the great god Shiva, who alone can grant him the powerful weapon he seeks.

By repeatedly drawing attention throughout the poem to the hero as a paradoxical figure, a warrior practicing asceticism, Bhavari imbues *Arjuna* with a dramatic tension that is nearly unique in the history of court epic. Bharavi presents the warrior-ascetic as a conundrum to be confronted and resolved. How can a warrior harness the peaceful means of self-discipline to achieve violent ends? How can a man be an active hero and a self-controlled yogi at the same time? Descriptions of asceticism and combat together illuminate Arjuna as an ideal warrior. The poem ends with a vision of Arjuna "towering over all the worlds with the innate courage of a warrior, and blazing with the fire of austerity"—harmoniously uniting qualities that merely appeared to be contradictory.[10]

INDRA TESTS ARJUNA

Pleased with Arjuna's anger against his enemies, a great
    warrior's inborn attribute, and equally pleased with
    his success in restraining the senses, Indra came to the
    hero's hermitage.[11]
The god took on the guise of an aged man fatigued by a
    long journey and appeared before his handsome son
    living the life of a hermit. His tawny mass of matted
    hair was everywhere sprinkled with gray, like the
    evening twilight mingled with the moon's rays. The
    wrinkled corners of his eyes, shaded by white
    eyebrows, made him look like a lake where the petals
    of lotuses are wilted by hoarfrost. Potbellied in spite
    of an emaciated frame, he leaned heavily on a staff,
    as if on a devoted wife. Even through this disguise he
    radiated a light that overpowered the world, like the
    sun barely veiled by a thin layer of clouds. His aged yet
    superhuman figure eclipsed the beauty of the
    hermitage, filling it with fear.
Pritha's son was overwhelmed by affection upon seeing
    Indra. The sight of a kinsman brings joy to one's heart
    even if he goes unrecognized.

After accepting the rites of hospitality offered by his son,
　　Indra pretended to rest on his seat, and then he spoke.

"You do well to practice austerities at this tender age. As a
　　rule, even elderly men like me are seduced by sensual
　　enjoyments.
Your handsome figure is made all the more handsome by
　　your virtue. Physical beauty is easily found in the
　　world, but a virtuous man is a rare thing indeed.
The charms of youth are as transient as the shadow of an
　　autumn cloud. The objects of the senses may please
　　for a while, but in the end they only torment.
Death is the destined end of man, who is constantly beset
　　by misfortune. Convinced that the cycle of birth and
　　death is a condition to be cast off, the worthy man
　　applies himself to the goal of liberation.
Your excellent resolve tells me that you are a man of
　　understanding. It is only your incongruous attire that
　　makes my heart doubt.
Why are you clad in armor, as though you were ready for
　　battle? Ascetics wear only deerskin and bark.
If you are truly a person of detachment, seeking
　　liberation, with no interest in protecting your body
　　and no wish to harm living beings, why do you carry a
　　fierce bow and two great quivers? And if you are
　　indeed the ascetic that you claim to be, this sword of
　　yours, as terrifying to mortals as a third arm of the god
　　of death, fails to convince me of your commitment to
　　nonviolence.

There is no doubt that victory over your enemies is your
ultimate goal. What does an ascetic, a man of peace,
have to do with weapons, symbols of rage?

He who turns actions designed to engender liberation into
means of slaughter is as foolish as the man who
muddies pure water, sole remedy for the malady of
thirst.

Do not cultivate wealth and desire, root causes of violence
and other evils! Both are insurmountable obstacles to
insight into the true nature of things.

The man who amasses transient wealth by injuring
creatures becomes a receptacle for all misfortunes,
like the ocean for all rivers.

As with misfortunes, so it is with riches; nothing about
them does not lead to pain. A man cannot deal with
either without the support of good friends. Both exact
exhausting labor, and both are a constant source of
fear.

Sensual pleasures are like the coils of a snake, terrible,
intractable enemies of the contentment that comes
from freedom from anxiety. Whoever pursues them is
sure to be ruined.

Riches are not discriminating; no one is really dear to
them. But fools become attached to riches. What
perverse creatures men are!

Nothing would detract from the praise of riches if they
were fickle only toward those without virtue, but
wealth is unscrupulous enough to cast aside even men
of good conduct.

Parting from what you love and meeting with what you
dislike have pained your heart in former lives, and will
pain it again.

When a man is in the company of loved ones, poverty
becomes plenty, misfortune turns into a festival, and
even being deceived seems like a favor.

When a man has been deprived of what he holds dear,
pleasant things become unpleasant, dear life itself
becomes a thorn, and, for all the friends he may have,
he is left utterly alone.

When you possess the beneficial things you desire, you are
wild with joy; when you lose them, you are tormented.
If you dislike pain for your own self, then do not let
yourself become the cause of another's pain.

You know that the human condition is as unstable as
fortune. So do not destroy what is right, for good men
depend on righteous conduct.

Give up your determination for war, do not utterly destroy
your great ascetic power. Cleave to peace, ascetic, so
that you may destroy the cycle of birth!

Conquer the enemies in your body, so difficult to
overcome—the senses, beginning with the eye. When
you have subdued these, you will have conquered the
whole world.

A man intent on amassing wealth, with no control of his
senses, shameless, and given to base deeds, becomes a
slave to other men, no better than an ox.

Today's pleasurable experience will fade into mere
memory tomorrow. Understand that desires are like
dreams; do not fall a prey to them!

Sensual pleasures win one's trust and yet are deceitful,
    pleasant yet the cause of pain, and hard to give up
    even when they depart of their own accord—they are
    perverse enemies indeed!
On this secluded mountain peak, perennially bathed by
    the river Ganga, Jahnu's daughter, liberation will
    come to you very soon. Put aside your weapons!"

With this, the lord of the storm gods ended his speech.
    Then Arjuna, hero with the monkey banner, delivered
    a speech dignified by courtesy.

"Your speech is pleasingly clear, yet complex; brief, yet
    profound; tightly constructed, yet not elliptical; of
    wide implication, yet not confused.
Since it is firmly founded on the tenets of logic, it appears
    to be independent of scripture; and yet, because it is
    irrefutable, it strikes the hearer as having the
    authority of scripture.
Since it cannot be overcome by opponents, it is powerful
    as the stormy ocean, yet through its thoughtful
    nobility and its success in achieving its goal, it is
    tranquil as the mind of a sage.
Could a speaker who does not possess your qualities of
    mind have made so pleasing a speech, endowed with
    so many good figures of speech and so well suited to
    the occasion?
Father, you do not know the circumstance of my
    undertaking, and that is why you seek to instruct me
    in a code of conduct proper to ascetics![12]

The words of one unaware of the context of his topic—he
    might be Brihaspati, lord of speech, himself—become
    as useless as the efforts of a warrior who defies
    political wisdom.
Father, well intentioned as they are, your words are no
    more appropriate for me than a starlit sky for the day.
I am a warrior, Dhanamjaya, son of Pandu by Pritha, and I
    stand at the command of my eldest brother, who has
    been exiled from his kingdom by our kinsmen, our
    rivals.[13]
At the command of the sage Krishna Dvaipayana, I have
    taken up this mode of life, the practice of austerity,
    focusing my efforts on propitiating Indra, whose favor
    is easily won.
The king, gambling with loaded dice in a rigged match,
    wagered his kingdom, himself, us, his brothers, and
    his wife. Such, I suppose, was our destiny.
In my absence he passes the long watches of the nights
    tormented by grief, along with his younger brothers
    and Draupadi.
Our enemies shamed us in the assembly, taking our upper
    robes by force, and then cutting us with wounding
    words.
The god of death put the notion into our enemies' hearts
    of disrobing the virtuous Draupadi, dark lady, in the
    presence of our elders, as if she were to become the
    security, taken in advance, for the Pandavas' paying
    up what they had lost.[14]
The courtiers could look at her only for a moment, as she
    entered the assembly hall, dragged by Duhshasana—

she was like the shadow, turning back, of a great tree
as it faces the evening sun.[15]

'What use is it to look at your husbands, whose actions
belie their title of *pati*, "husband, protector?"'—it was
as if with this in mind that her eyes blurred with tears.

It was the eldest among us, a lover of virtue, who tolerated
our final disgrace, for it is easy to defeat one's enemies,
but hard to retain one's good name among good men.

The waters of oceans and the minds of honorable men are
averse to overstepping their bounds and remain pure
even when agitated.

It was our very friendship with the sons of Dhritarashtra
that generated their enmity toward us. Associating
with bad men, like resorting to a crumbling riverbank
for shelter, is sure to end in disaster.

A scoundrel's actions are as unfathomable as the ways of
fate, for both are unafraid of ill repute and indifferent
to virtue and vice.

My heart would have instantly burst to be overpowered by
enemies in this way, had not my indignation given me
the thought of revenge to rely upon.

Ousted by the enemy, we have been forced to live like deer
in the forest. We are ashamed even to face one
another, much less our friends.

A man who has lost his pride suffers the fate of a blade of
grass, bowed down for want of strength, and of no
consequence because of a lack of substance.

It is not surprising that great men treasure loftiness, for
they have learned that the highest parts of a mountain
are the most difficult to scale.

Only so long does prosperity accompany a man, only so
long does his fame endure, only so long is he a real
man, as he does not lose his honor.

That man is born to some purpose, if the finger that is
raised to count his name as first among men is never
followed by another finger.[16]

A mountain, however high, and grown over with
impenetrable forests, can still be scaled; but a man of
great prowess, dignified with pride, can never be
overcome.

It is such men, whose bright fame shames the moon's orb,
who dignify their descendants with their name;
through them the earth becomes fit to be called
vasumdharā, she who bears riches.[17]

They are the examples used in benedictions, the foremost
among men of self-respect, whose wrath strikes their
enemies as a thunderbolt strikes a dead tree.

I do not crave the pleasures of sense, nor wealth, unsteady
as the waves of the ocean; nor do I seek the
sequestered haven of liberation, out of fear of that
thunderbolt, the transience of human existence. I seek
instead to wash away, with the tears of our enemy's
grieving widows, the mud of disgrace that treachery
has heaped upon us!

I do not care if I become the butt of ridicule for good men
or if this undertaking is an error of judgment on my
part. So do not feel too chagrined at having aimed
your efforts at persuasion at an unsuitable target!

Until I exterminate my enemies and restore the reputation
of my family, I shall think of liberation itself as an
obstacle to victory!

So long as a man has not regained through his arrows the
fame seized by his enemies, he is as good as if he had
not been born, as if he were dead, as if he were a mere
blade of grass.

If a man's indignation can be stilled before he has defeated
his enemy, how can he still be called a man? Tell me,
sage, yourself!

Of what use is it to call him a man who is a man by mere
accident of birth? That man alone is worthy of being
called such who is spoken of with admiration by men
who treasure virtue, and whose name, uttered with
awe in the assembly of men, overpowers other men
and draws praise even from his enemies.

Seeking to fulfill his vow of taking revenge on his enemies
in war, the king has placed his hopes in me, like a
thirsty man in a handful of water.

That man is a blot on his noble family, like the spot on the
moon, who fails, when hard times come, to carry out
his master's command.

What is more, how can I take up renunciation before its
due time, a course that would interfere with the code
of conduct laid down for me? The ancient lawgivers
teach us to take the stages of life in order, and not to
violate their sequence.[18]

This tremendous yoke has fallen upon my shoulders; my
mother too is far away, my brother is my king, elder to

me and very pious—all these things constrain my
freedom to choose.

Self-respecting men stand by the code of conduct
appropriate for them and do not transgress it. Even
when crushed by the enemy, they do not flee from
battle.

I shall either propitiate Indra, god with the thousand eyes,
and pluck out the thorn of dishonor, or perish upon
this mountain peak, like a shattered cloud."[19]

When Arjuna fell silent, Indra the bounteous revealed his
own divine form and gathered his son into his
embrace. He then instructed the hero to propitiate
Shiva, source of birth and death, by means of
austerities that destroy evil, with the aim of winning
supreme power.

"When you have pleased Shiva the archer with heroic
deeds enabled by myself and the guardian gods of the
worlds—deeds that will remain unmatched in all three
worlds—you will win back royal fortune from your
enemies." With this, the god vanished.

3.

Selections from
The Life of Harishchandra

by Raghavanka

Translated from Kannada
by Vanamala Vishwanatha

The Life of Harishchandra is a narrative poem composed in 1225 by
Raghavanka, a poet associated with the court of King Devaraja in
Hampi, a town in northern Karnataka.[1] Raghavanka was born into
a Brahman family with a poetic lineage in Pampapura, or Hampi,
on the banks of the Tungabhadra River. His exact dates have been
long debated, but he most likely lived from about 1185 to 1235.

Although the title of the work is *The Life of Harishchandra*
(*Hariśchandra Cāritra*), it has become celebrated in Kannada cul-
ture as *Hariścandra Kāvyam,* literally "The Poem of Harishchan-
dra," which speaks to its expressive and imaginative power. The
first work to turn this ancient Indian legend into a full-fledged po-
etic composition, it tells the engrossing tale of the dispossession
and deprivation of King Harishchandra, who suffered for his com-
mitment to one paramount value, truthfulness.

The poem has remained alive in both high literary culture and popular imagination since the thirteenth century. It reached Kannada-speaking homes through the oral traditions. It was further disseminated through traditional arts, theater performances, and films such as *Satya Hariścandra* (1965) and the first Indian film ever made, *Rāja Hariścandra* (1913), based on this legend. Even the centrality of truth in Gandhi's thought and life might be traced back to the Harishchandra play he saw as a child, an experience that remained deeply etched in his mind.[2]

The story of King Harishchandra has its roots in the ancient Vedas and is widely attested in Sanskrit puranic literature.[3] Irrespective of variations in plot, structure, genre, and worldview, all Harishchandra narratives share the common theme of a virtuous king who is compelled to sacrifice all that he holds dear when those values clash with truthfulness. While Vedic sources highlight the story's elements of ritual sacrifice and the later Puranas foreground its historical aspects, literary versions focus on the ethical dilemma of the protagonist. However, prior to *Hariścandra Kāvyam* no single text included all these elements in a unified, organic, and detailed narrative. Raghavanka rewrote the puranic legend as a Kannada text comprising 728 verses and divided into two parts that reflect the ups and downs of Harishchandra's life: after the conventional opening chapter locates the poet and the work in their context, the following six chapters offer an account of Harishchandra's ascent, and the next six describe his descent, with the concluding chapter recounting his restoration to the throne.

Raghavanka made crucial changes in diction, plot, structure, genre, and ideological thrust by inflecting his text with the anxieties and tensions that marked his own sectarian and literary identity. He effected this transformation so naturally and with such finesse that critics have said Harishchandra sounds altogether like a Kannada king.[4]

Raghavanka was also a trendsetter in matters of literary form. His achievement in prosody, for example, prompted later poets to use *dēsi,* or regional, meters especially the six-line *ṣaṭpadi*—a unique prosody evolved from popular poetry, "poetry to be sung" (*hāḍug-abba*)—rather than metrical conventions derived from the Sanskrit tradition.[5] As a literary form, *ṣaṭpadi* had found scattered mention in earlier texts on poetics, but Raghavanka was the first to deploy it as a full-fledged form for an entire text and composed all his works in this meter. Additionally, the particular tone and tenor of the spoken language of Raghavanka's region can be heard in the profusion of proverbs and everyday speech rhythms in the text.[6] Since he used the local idiom to create an accessible yet exalted style, his poetry spoke to people with an astonishing immediacy.

The universal ideal of truth speaking—which transcends boundaries of caste, community, and language—in the Sanskrit texts is transformed here into a particular vision of truth located in the caste-based Kannada socio-religious world of the thirteenth century. One fnds a range of responses to Raghavanka's treatment of political, religious, and cultural issues. He is at times praised as a progressive for raising radical questions about caste and other normative Hindu practices in a milieu hostile to such questioning.[7] Equally, he has been sharply criticized for not being radical enough, and for endorsing inhuman practices of caste and gender violence through valorizing kingship, for his implicit endorsement of caste purity and untouchability, and for not transcending the limits of his social reality.[8] While there is no critical consensus, what comes across unambiguously is Raghavanka's ability to speak to the burning issues of power, caste, and gender, not only of his times but equally of contemporary India.

In transmuting Harishchandra, who is portrayed as a liar in the Vedas, into an icon of truth, by drawing a vivid picture of Harishchandra as a devout king who single-mindedly pursues truth as an integral part of his being, Raghvanka has made the epithet of truthfulness, *satya,* an indissoluble part of the king's name in Kannada culture: Satya Harishchandra.

THE FOREST FIRE

On the strength of the spiritual merit he had accrued, Harishchandra successfully overcomes the destructive forest fire conjured up by Vishvamitra and finally reaches the city of Kashi.

Harishchandra resumed his journey, after washing his hands and feet in the pond, offering evening oblations, worshiping moon-crested Shiva's feet, praying to his gurus, and partaking of the *prasāda.*[9] As he watched the forest in amazement, he was courage personified, carrying his son, talking to his beloved wife and his minister, and conversing with Nakshatraka, the dues collector.

The top of his head burning from the scorching sun, the soles of his feet from the heat of the ground, his body from the enveloping hot breeze, his stomach from fiery hunger, and his mouth from parching thirst, Harishchandra walked on, dragging his feet in agony. How do I describe what awaited him ahead, all owing to the terrible cunning of that heartless sage?

Suddenly he saw all around them huge elephants with their tusks on fire; birds with their feathers on fire; big and small animals on fire; thick, mature clumps of trees on fire; tribal women with their peacock-feather dresses on fire; bears with their fur on fire; and hunters on fire—all of them rushing toward them, screaming. How do I praise the king's brave attempt to dodge the onrush of burning carcasses and move on with the queen?

Was it the angry fire spewed by the son of sage Bhṛgu, who had been killed by Kritavirya, progeny of Vishvavasu?[10] Had this fire, not content even after drinking up the entire ocean, then turned its ire on earth by burning everything in its wake? Or was it the fire of ultimate annihilation that Rudra had beckoned with a wave of his hand? As Harishchandra wondered, the fire raged on.

Burning down thick clumps of bamboo,
cleaving through mighty mountains, their wings severed,
blackening the ground overgrown with thick shrubs,
and blowing through hollows of gigantic trees,
the fire blazed through the forest...
searing and smoking and sizzling and spiraling...
soaring to the skies and scattering...
striking from every side...
the forest fire enveloped Harishchandra,
himself, a forest fire to the forest of untruth.

41

Bhugibhugil bhugibhugil*... chiḷichiḷil chiṭichiṭil...
dhagadhagil dhagadhagil...gharigharil ghari gharil...
dhagadhagam dhagadhagam dhagadhagil...
chimichimil churuchuril chaṭachaṭa...
dhamdhaga dhagadhagam...ghuḷughuḷu...
the fire swelled... splintering... springing like a creeper...
its blazing flame turning everything black... spewing black
    smoke...
red sparks flying in all directions...
the fire engulfed the forest on all four sides.

The enveloping fire, was it the fire of the collective sorrow
of people mourning for their slain kings, a sorrow that had
bided its time and now found vent? Or was it the dues
collector's way of warning, "Do not take one step more;
pay up first," by drawing this circle of fire around Harish-
chandra? Or was it a ring of fire created by the sun around
his descendant to protect him?

Fearing the worst, the king grasped the hands of his wife
and child firmly, urging them on: "Don't stop... keep
moving... or it will kill us... move... run now..." Seeing the
fire rushing at them from all sides, he desperately looked
around for ways to escape from its crushing arms. All of a
sudden, he found himself surrounded by hordes of birds and
animals, some half dead, some writhing in pain, and some
dying from the burns.

* Sounds of the fire.

Burning and burning,
burning the snake's hood, burning the *sāraṅga* buck's ribs,
lion's mane, tiger's head, gaur's ears, deer's legs,
fox's face, wolf's snout, rabbit's stomach, doe's shanks,
wild buffalo's tail, wild boar's high thighs, and hound's
    flanks...
burning and burning, seared and scorched,
they hurtled upon the king, senseless.
How do I describe this horrific sight!

The king gaped at the scene open-mouthed:
If you escape the elephant, the tiger is lying in wait;
dodge the tiger, the bear grunts in your ear;
back off, the serpent comes at you;
turn around, the lion roars next to you;
move a step, the wild boar comes charging;
slink away, the deer comes butting;
then, the gaur is all set to pounce on you;
next, the buck is ready for you with its sharp horns;
and, if you are alive still, the wild bull is out to crush you!
His wife and son were just as dumbstruck.

While the king and his companions were busy keeping
the animals at bay and trying to move out of their range,
the gods in heaven, watching the uncontainable forest fire
grow relentlessly in every direction, were deeply disturbed
by the king's plight. They pleaded with Shiva urgently,
"Oh Lord Shiva! Mahadeva! See how the whole forest has
turned into a blaze...Look how it is burning...breaking

out everywhere … annihilating everything … Have mercy, protect King Harishchandra! We beg of you, Oh Lord."

Did he break or blanch? Did he shrink or shirk? Did he dither or diminish? The king, even in the face of that inferno, shone like the sun surrounded by the aura of the eastern sky; he was radiant like Mrida, who withstood the venomous *kālakūṭa* poison emanating from the churned ocean, strong enough to annihilate all the three worlds; he was effulgent like God surrounded by the rich light of pure and eternal knowledge.

"I have not yet reached Kashi; I have not yet paid back my debt to the sage; I have not stepped out of the borders of the land I gave away; nor have I completed my full span of life. If I alone were to die, that is one thing; but I am dragging down the lives of my wife, child, and the minister as well. Oh, what a terrible way to die, in this infernal fire!" Haunted by these anxieties, the king bemoaned his plight.

"Instead of assuaging Yama's hunger in the battlefield, provoking Mari's disgust, ending the drought of Death's mouth, making those terrible ghosts and goblins throw up, slaking the thirst of the sword's edge, slaying my enemies until the itch in my arms is stilled, and lolling on the head of the royal elephant as if one was resting on the breasts of Mukti, goddess of liberation, and enjoying pleasures matching those of Indra, here I am being consumed in a fire. Oh, what a pity!"

Thick, black smoke engulfed them, the fire blazed right next to them, red sparks splattered all over, and cinders exploded in their face. In utter misery, the king poured out his woes to the minister: "How can I see my loved ones scream in agony as their bodies are charred and their skin peels off, and watch them die? I do not want to die after them; I would rather fall into this fire right away. Do not stop me, do not grieve for me."

Satyakirti begged the king, hands folded, "There can be no worse sinner than one who has to watch his master die. Could that ever be a virtuous deed? What is the point of my holding onto life when you have gone? I would rather die before you so that my reputation as a loyal servant will be intact. Would a servant ever let his king walk ahead? Hence, speak no more like this, my lord."

"A high-born man; a great Brahman; a scholar of the Vedas, learned in the scriptures; a devout Shaiva; an elder with a head of gray hair, you have followed me, giving up your own family. Can I push you into this raging fire and walk into the most horrific of hells? How can I bear the infamy of such an act? Stop, not one step further! Swear to me," said the king, dissuading his minister.

Then his son pleaded: "It is said that if one offers to the fire a young boy, innocent of the pleasures of the world, it will be appeased and its fury will abate. So if you sacrifice me to the fire, it is bound to protect all of you. So send me off right away, Father."

The king said, "You cannot go; you are yet to experience the pleasures of the throne."

The son countered: "But the throne has been made over to Kaushika. Where is the kingdom to rule?"

"Do you not know of Dhruva, King Uttanapada's son, who after being pushed off the king's lap by his stepmother, Suruchi, turned to penance and pleased lord Shiva, who gave him the fourteen worlds to rule over? There is always Shiva who will give; you are there to humbly take it; you will have the good fortune of being king. So, you cannot go my son," said the king.

"What is the point of going on like this? The raging fire is rushing at us. Please permit me to sacrifice myself, my lord," said the exemplary queen. And Harishchandra said, "How can I? What I most devoutly wish is for people to say that the king, even after having lost all his marvelous wealth, protected his beloved wife until his last breath. I will not earn the infamy of being a coward who, fearing for his own life, pushed his wife into the towering fires. I simply cannot."

"Oh my lord, would this fire kill me alone and spare all of you? It is not proper for me to die along with you; it is a sin to live after you; I would rather die the chosen, supreme death of a chaste wife who precedes her husband in death. I beg you to let me go first." Thus Chandramati, proud of her status as a dedicated wife, fell at his feet, and coaxed and cajoled the king to let her go first.

Suppressing the sorrow boiling within, the king gave his consent. Chandramati bowed at his feet to take her leave.

When he saw this, his son, Lohitashva, started crying. Tugging at her sari, he demanded, "Where are you going, Mother? I am going with you." Wiping the tears from his cheeks and cuddling him, she consoled him, "Don't cry, my pet. I'll come back soon."

Prostrating herself before her husband, she said:
"Proud to have a loving husband who indulges my every
    wish,
I have often taken liberties in your royal presence—
not cared enough and not loved enough,
not been timorous enough nor reverent enough,
and not received you with due courtesy;
I may have dared to sit on the same throne.
I may have talked back, and even berated you.
Forgive me all my transgressions, my lord."
Bidding farewell to all, she stood facing the fire.

Bowing in every direction,
she offered her respects to the sun and prayed:
"May Harishchandra be my husband a million lives to
    come.
May Lohitashva be born as my son again.
May elder Satyakirti ever remain the minister.
May the moon-crested lord be my god forever.
May Vishvamitra who now rules our earth be eternal.

"Hear me, lord of earth!
If I do not hail from two pure lineages,
if I have ever thought of anyone else but you,

if I have ever fed you one thing and eaten another thing
    myself,
if I have ever prayed in body, mind, and soul to gods other
    than Shiva,
then may Agni, this forest fire, consume me alive.
If not, may this fire let up and give way."
How do I describe this moment,
a witness to the potent words of a chaste wife?

At that point, as if to frighten the young woman, the fire
raged even higher, leaping to the skies. Unruffled, she walked
in ... in ... into the consuming fire. Oh Shiva, Shiva ... Ma-
hadeva! When she walked into it without caring a whit, what
should happen! It looked as though the sun itself had entered
pitch darkness; the spurious fire caused by the sage Kaushika
took flight and vanished. How far can guile and cunning re-
sist the power of the virtuous?

The gods in heaven rained down flowers that cooled the heat
of the earth. Stunned by her undaunted strength of charac-
ter and purity, the ecstatic king embraced his wife; the min-
ister knelt before her; and the son jumped in joy. Thanks to
Shiva's benevolence, the threat of fire disappeared just as it
had appeared.

    The time set by the harsh sage was fast approaching. So
they decided to quickly cross the Vindhya ranges.

Ranging through many cities, countless forests, and nu-
merous mountains, they finally sighted the Ganga. The

resplendent river flowed mellifluously, announcing to the people of the earth: "I am the destroyer of mounds of defilement accrued through a hundred *kali* eons;[11] I am the moonlight that shines over millions and millions of sinning lotuses; I am the bolt of lightning that grinds to dust the mountains of fear of rebirth."

The river sent out soft, shining wavelets, as if ruing her impulse to flow over and submerge. One moment, the waves danced their way to the banks melodiously, and the next, a sudden swell of water flooded in thunderously, bringing in white, bubbly waves. How do I describe the wondrous play of these magical waves?

The Ganga!
Listening to her very name destroys all sins; thinking of
     her brings spiritual gain;
talking of her fulfills all aspirations; sighting her ends all
     births and rebirths;
praising her brings one Indra's title; touching her affords
     one Brahma's stature.
If you cup your hand and drink her, you will attain
     salvation;
if you submerge yourself in her, you will attain the status
     of Ganesha;
and if you approach her, you will reach the status of Maha
     Rudratva.[12]
The Vedas bear witness to this power of the Ganga.

She is replete with waves *(bhaṅga)*,[13]
yet saves the humble from humiliation *(bhaṅga)*;
she is inclined to flow downward *(adhōgamane)*,
yet leads those who touch her upward *(ūrdhvagamana)*;
she is always unfavorable *(pratikūle)*,[14]
yet she is favorable *(anukūle)* to those who drink her
    waters;
she is venom-bodied *(viṣadēhi)*,
yet blesses her devotees with a nectar-body *(amṛtadēha)*.
Oh Ganga, what a medley of opposites!

After their ritual bath in the Ganga, Harishchandra and his companions crossed the river, which made them feel as though they had crossed over the fearful ocean of rebirth. The Ganga swelled, knowing she was rid of the accumulated sins washed away in her waters by the wicked, and was purified, since a devoted wife like Chandramati, a worthy king who spoke no untruth, a child who belonged to two pure lineages, and a minister who was dedicated to his king had all purified her by their touch.

Harishchandra felt doubly blessed having bathed in the Ganga, since her divinity can destroy the forest of sins committed by her devotees. It felt like drinking ambrosia after partaking of the life-giving herb, reposing on the philosopher's stone under the heavenly wish-granting tree, and holding the linga in your palm while being blessed by your guru. The worthy king entered the holy city of Kashi as easily as god's *prasāda* would go down his great devotees' throats.

Sun Street, radiant enough to destroy sins, and Moon Street lit up by moonlight, were both laid out with rows of buildings, matching wall designs, streamers, shining golden cupolas, and marble walls that followed a common layout, and in their midst stood the temple of Lord Vishvanatha, the abode of Shiva, with an aura that was not of this world.

While most pilgrim centers offer either pleasure or spiritual gain, Kashi offers both, true to the adage, "Properly ministered, even venom can be good medicine." Who will pass up the chance if the holy water one drinks can turn fragrant? Who would want to miss an opportunity if the *prasāda* one partakes of could turn into sweetened rice? The spiritual center of Kashi was the kind of extraordinary place that served people in the here and in the hereafter, equally.

The holy city of Kashi was known for its spiritual powers that could keep at bay famine, mutiny, pestilence, sin, the love god's passion, carnal desire, and all the preternatural forces. The king was fascinated by Kashi, which had offered the lord a resting place and become famous as the abode of Shiva. He marveled at the city so replete with divine energy.

As the king moved farther into the city, he could discern in the distance, under the shade of a host of fluttering flags, the cupola of the Vishvanatha temple, an auspicious and pleasing sight. It shone like the ruby-studded crown of the goddess of liberation, seated in her distinguished throne above and holding court amid yak-tail fans, in the expanse of heaven.

51

The Vyasahasta—that imposing crown of bamboo, rounded like a trunk—was an outstretched hand, raised to declare that there was no god equal to our lord of the universe, the slayer of Madana, in all the fourteen worlds. It was a hand of reassurance, saying "Do not fear" to sinners, and a hand beckoning those who were seeking spiritual solace and uplift.

Harishchandra was mesmerized by the countless Nandi* flags that leaped high and triumphant, piercing through the womb of the sky; the golden cupolas that outshone the radiance of a million suns; the majesty of imposing temples of Shiva; and the thronging crowds of devotees chanting and singing Shiva's praise, worshiping and prostrating themselves in front of Shiva's image. As he made his way through the happy and elated crowds, he beheld Vishvanatha, lord of the universe.

His eyes riveted on the effulgence of the lord,
Harishchandra sang the praises of the auspicious Shiva:
Hail the lord revered by Vishnu;
Hail the lord venerated by Brahma;
Hail the lord, protector of Indra who slayed Jambha;
Hail the lord beyond all worship;
Hail the fiery-eyed, Ganga-crested lord;
Hail the lord, conqueror of Madana, untouched by birth
 and death;
Hail the lord, moving force of the universe;

----

* The bull, Shiva's mount.

Hail the lord, foe of sinners worshiping other gods;
Hail the lord, omnipresent and victorious!

Beholding the god's image, the king was ecstatic:
praising, singing, praying for greater devotion,
communing with the lord,
imploring, gratefully partaking of the *prasāda*,
detaching himself from his trying circumstances,
and crossing the ocean of this materialist world,
the king returned from the temple in a state of bliss,
gazing at the other images of the linga
as a new strength fortified his being.

Once, sage Durvasa came for the wedding of Shrimati,*
along with Narada and Parvata, who vied with each other
to marry the beautiful princess. Taken up by the genius of
the place, Durvasa stayed on in Kashi and undertook a severe
penance to have Shiva appear before him. But as he waited
for Lord Shiva to grant him his wish, he grew impatient and
was about to utter the curse that the city of Kashi should
lose its sacred powers. Shiva appeared at that point, urging
him not to curse Kashi. Put to shame by his own petulance,
Durvasa offered special prayers to the moon-crested lord of
Kama, and reverentially set up the image of Kamesha, Lord
of Wishes, sanctifying Kashi. Harishchandra bowed to this
Kamesha in utter humility!

---

* Daughter of Ambarisha, king of Ayodhya.

53

The power of Kashi is so incredible that even the worst sinners are said to turn into the linga. Once an ascetic went after the wife of a fisherman; when he was faced with a hostile crowd, terrified, he hid inside a *vibhāṇḍa,* a huge, round vessel. Unaware of this, the fisherman filled the vessel with spirits. People expected to see the dead ascetic in the circular vessel; instead, they found the image of a linga inside! The king had a glimpse of Vibhandesha, lord of the *vibhāṇḍa,* in total amazement.

Once King Daksha, who was conducting a fire sacrifice, saw Vireshvara issuing forth from Shiva's fiery, third eye, thundering and slaughtering the gods that were part of the sacrifice. He was shaken as never before. To make amends for the transgression of conducting a fire sacrifice without praying to Lord Shiva, Daksha mounted the image of Lord Shiva. Harishchandra beheld this Daksheshvara in absolute awe.

As Harishchandra gazed in rapt admiration at the divine beauty of the lingas, their rich depth, their aura of goodness, and their formal elegance, he completely lost himself in that exquisite ambience and forgot his own hardships. Suddenly Nakshatraka materialized in front of him like Mari. He demanded, pulling at the king's clothes, "Hand me the money, now. If you delay, my master will get wild with me. Give it to me right away.

"If you're going to spend your time worshiping every god on the way, one month will not be enough time. I have somehow managed until now. The time given to you, in fact, ends today. Give me the money now; if you do not, your claim to truth will end right away." The heartless Nakshatraka pushed them out on the street, blocked their movements, and made them stand under the scorching sun, which beat down mercilessly upon them.

4.

Selections from
The Story of Manu

by Allasani Peddana

*Translated from Telugu
by Velcheru Narayana Rao
and David Shulman*

Allasani Peddana confidently calls himself the "creator of Telugu poetry" (*āndhrakavitāpitāmaha*),[1] and generations of his readers, including his own patron, King Krishnadevaraya, accepted this description.

We know when this poet lived and worked—roughly around 1520, at the height of the power of Krishnadevaraya, who ruled from 1509 to 1529 in Vijayanagara, the capital of the last imperial state system in premodern south India. These two figures, king and poet, were very closely intertwined. We can think of Peddana as Krishnadevaraya's primary court poet and his book, *The Story of Manu* (*Manucaritramu*), as the epitome of this vital, expansive moment in all cultural and political domains. To no small degree, Peddana's book embodies the ethos and creative vision of Vijayanagara at its height.

Peddana became, for later generations, the archetype of the true poet, like Kalidasa for Sanskrit and Kampan for Tamil. In a wider, comparative perspective, we might think of Peddana, like Dante, as the epitome of an entire civilizational moment.

"Creator"—*pitāmaha,* literally "grandfather"—is a word applied to Brahma, the god who creates the world in the sense of forming and shaping in his imagination the stuff of potential reality.[2] But Peddana's appropriation of the term has a different, far more specific connotation. He crafted a new kind of poetry and a new kind of book, one never seen before in Telugu.

Peddana writes in an unprecedented style, marked by distinctive qualities of complexity and intensity on all levels—thematic, lexical, syntactic, metrical, musical, and so on. He shows us a first-order "written-ness." His poems are syntactically complex, with carefully chiseled phrases, as well as complex repetition. The adjective "lyrical" comes to mind: a musical tuning that results from contemplative crafting of the line.

Poetry, from this point on, is a matter of personal, private experience. We could call such poetry *pāṭhya,* "to be read for oneself," as opposed to the classical Sanskrit division into *dṛśya,* "visible" (that is, dramatic literature), and *śravya,* "audible" (that is, publicly read).[3] The new category has a thematic implication since *The Story of Manu,* like most of the other major Telugu poetic works of the sixteenth century, is powerfully focused on human interiority—the workings and contents of the human mind and the expression and exploration of self.

Here we also see a fascination with real things that make up the world and shape life in the world, meticulously observed and reported by the poet at a level of high resolution. Nothing like this kind of hyperrealistic description had ever been seen before in Sanskrit or, for that matter, in other south Indian languages. Such total commitment to a rather modern realism coexists with an interest in the fantastic and the magical, including boldly imagined events in the worlds of gods and gandharvas.

The Story of Manu takes as its theme the birth of Manu/Man. The story was known before, both in Sanskrit and in Telugu, but its elaboration and reconceptualization belong to this historical moment. The whole book, on one level, is an extended essay on the making of a full human being and, by the end, of a fully human king.

As the story unfolds, an innocent but restless Brahman is transported to the Himalayas, where a divine woman falls in love with him and offers herself to him in vain. He departs. His image, however, remains fixed, indeed burning like fire, in her mind.

After this meeting, Peddana traces generations to Manu's birth. There is also a conventional frame for the text, where the patron, Krishnadevaraya, listens to a story originally told by the sage Markandeya to another sage, Kroshti; this narration was then repeated by a group of learned and articulate birds speaking to the sage Jaimini. No one ever tells the story for the first time, and there are always two and only two roles—narrator and listener—sequentially occupied over several generations and dialogically linked.

The Story of Manu tells us about the making of a good king, in a good world, from the disparate pieces of experience that conduce toward this goal over three generations. It also shows us, not in some theoretical or abstract manner but in practice and felt experience and language commensurate with such feeling, what it takes for anyone to become fully human.

THE SIDDHA'S GIFT

For Krishnaraya, son of Narasimha and the grandson of
Ishvara, wishing him an always escalating happiness,
I am composing this book called
"The Birth of Svarochisha Manu."

If you'd like to know how the story unfolds, listen.
After hearing the story of Svayambhuva Manu, Jaimini
    asked the wise birds,
"After him, who was the next Manu?⁴ Tell me, please." The
    birds began to speak,
just as Markandeya had once told the story to Kroshti.

There was a city called Arunaspada in the country where
    good people live,
on the banks of the Varana River. Its citadel kissed the sky,
and its houses were painted so white that they washed
    away
the dark spot on the moon. It shone like a pendant
on the neck of Lady Earth.

The Brahmans there were so proud of their learning in
    all fields
that they disdained even Brahma, the first god, for
    growing senile.
The warriors were so tough they could send a servant
to summon even Rama of the ax to their presence.

The merchants were rich enough to put Kubera back in
    business
with a start-up loan if ever he went bankrupt.
The farmers prospered from their plows. They could give
    so much to Shiva,
the first beggar, that he'd never need to beg again.
The courtesans were so expert in dancing
that they could dismiss the most beautiful women from
    heaven
with a single flourish of their saris.
There even a budding branch was harder than iron.[5]

A man called Pravara lived in that city, never leaving it.
No painter could do justice to his beauty.
He was like the love god reborn. Handsome as the moon.
A great linguist. Intent on all kinds of rites
and duties. A jewel of a Brahman.
His one great love was to teach.

He was free from desire, so his beauty was totally
beyond the reach of any and all women
who wanted him, like the fragrance
of the champak flower for all hovering bees.[6]

Though young, he had already completed a Vedic rite.
He was rich too. He loved his wife.
The elders had measured the length of their hair
to be sure they were well matched.
She was the source of all his happiness.

His old parents, like Shiva and Parvati,
looked after the house.

You could see him every day walking from the river
with his students in tow carrying fruits, firewood,
darbha grass, flowers, and clean-washed clothes.
He'd get up at dawn, when the breeze from the Varana
carrying the sharp fragrance of half-open lotus flowers
caressed his body. He would chant the morning prayer
to Vishnu upon waking,[7] then bathe in the river
to cleanse himself of sins, perform
the dawn ritual, meditate on the Savitri mantra
and, standing on the riverbank, greet the rising sun
who sees everything.

He was good, born in the right family, gentle, disciplined,
young, and handsome. Many kings wanted to give him
        gifts,
but he accepted nothing, not even a *sālagrāma* stone.[8]
He had enough. His fields yielded everything he needed.
There was always plenty of milk and rice.

His wife never tired of cooking. She was like the goddess
of food, Annapurna. Even if a thousand guests turned up
late at night, she would feed them all they wanted.

But—he had always wanted to travel.
Anytime he heard that pilgrims had come from far away,
he'd rush to receive them, even at some distance,
and wash their feet and take them home,

and honor them as his guests and feed them
fine food and make them happy. Then, when they were
    seated
comfortably, he'd draw near and ask them all about
oceans, mountains, rivers, and places of power,
and exactly how far they were from his place.
Then he would sigh heavily: "Someday I should go
and see them." That young Brahman had fire
to tend at home.[9]

His whole life was given to serving unannounced guests.
One day, late in the afternoon,

a certain siddha, a specialist in herbs, arrived.
He wore a tiger's skin on his head, covering his red
    matted hair.
In his hand, circled by a five-metal bracelet, he carried
a bag and a yogi's stick to rest his arms.
A doeskin belt was tightly bound around his waist,
making his belly bulge. His thin body, shimmering like
    polished brass,
was covered with ash. A strap useful in yogic postures
was hanging from his broad chest, and *rudrākṣa* beads
dangled from his ears. He was dressed
in ochre, with a water pot
in one hand.

Pravara saw the great yogi
arriving and went toward him, bowed to him in reverence,

honored him with water to sip and to wash his feet,
and made him happy with delicious food.

Then he said: "Where are you coming from
and where are you headed? You are honored
by learned people, and I am honored
by your presence in my house today.

Whatever you say is a mantra.
Wherever you go is Prayaga.[10]
The water that washes your feet
duplicates on earth
the river from heaven.

When yogis like you come to visit,
bathe, eat, drink, and rest, and leave
in joy, the man of that house finds himself
lucky. He is really blessed, and truly fulfilled
in all ways. His life
is a life.

Householders like me,
mired in the cares of family life—
what can make us free other than the specks of dust
on the soles of your feet?"

The yogi answered him.
"Son, listen to me.
Your good life at home

is what sets pilgrims like us
free to move from place to place.

Honey from *taṅgeḍu* flowers nearby,
cash in your pocket,
the wish-giving tree, ripe with fruit, in your backyard,
the wish-giving cow in your pen,
a well you can walk into that never dries up,
a mountain of gold within reach,
a drink of cool water on a hot day,
a square meal when you're hungry—
a family man is all these to the deaf, lame, blind,
beggars and bachelors, renouncers, vagrants,
unannounced guests, monks, naked itinerants,
skull holders, and all other homeless people.
There's nothing like family life."

Now Pravara said: "Honored sir,
you've seen all the holy places.
Tell me something about each of them.

What are the countries you have visited? The mountains
you have climbed? The rivers you've bathed in?
The islands you've explored? The godly forests
you've entered? The oceans you have come to?
Tell me about all of them, in all their new
and wonderful details.

If I can't go there myself, the next best thing
is to hear about their power.

That will make me pure. That's why I'm asking you."
The siddha replied from his kind heart.

"You are like a full moon rising over the milky ocean
of Brahman families. Driven by the desire to visit
holy places, I've gone everywhere.
Seen everything—countries, rivers flowing
east and west, marvels of all kinds—in the space
between Sandal Mountain,[11] the Western Mountain,
Snow Mountain, and the Mountain of the East.

I worshiped the lord of Kedara. I put my head to the feet
of the goddess Hingula. I served Vishnu of the beautiful
    eyes
who lives in Prayaga. I saw Narayana at Badari,
married to the Ocean's daughter. Why mention this place
or that? I've seen everything under the sky.[12]

Let that be. Listen, my householder friend. On the sunrise
mountain, yaks crane their necks to catch a glimpse of the
splendid yak-tail banners that adorn the horses yoked to the
chariot of the rising sun. Could even the thousand-tongued
snake Adishesha count all the wonders of that place?

    Then there's Malaya Mountain to the south. It's a cool
place, priceless. That's where all the female snakes coil them-
selves around the sandalwood trees, enveloped by vines of
cardamom, to cool their fiery yearning for their husband,
who has taken up residence on Shiva's neck, far away.

    On the sunset mountain, the great elephant of the west

breaks off the buds of the *sallaki* branches that are soaked with a continuous drizzle of elixir dripping from the waning moon that lingers in the mountain passes and the crevices tucked among the tall peaks. If I think about how I used to rest there, seated on pedestals of precious stone, I break out in goose-bumps even now.

And you've no doubt heard of Silver Mountain, where elegant yaksha women come to hasten the blossoming of the trees they have nurtured, and the chiming of their anklets invites languid royal geese to join them. There are secret places there where black-neck Shiva enjoys his time with Parvati. Once you see those places, all the sorrows of existence will vanish.

The elephant Airavana,[13] continually in rut, strikes the mountain slopes with his tusks and digs up the bright red *kuravinda* flowers, and his mate, certain that she's seeing firebrands, retreats in fear. Such remarkable sights occur all the time on Mount Meru. Only a fortunate man whose karma has ripened over many births will be able to see them. I myself have seen all this in a very short span of time thanks to god's blessings." Pravara, with a little smile that swallowed up his cheeks, said to him:

"Forgive my boldness in asking. It would take years
and years to see all this, even if one had wings.
But I can tell just by looking at your face
that you're very young. How can someone like me
know your powers? Only you can know them.
What can I say?"

The stranger replied, "What's wrong in asking? Neither age nor sickness dares to touch us. We're siddhas.

It's a secret, but I'll tell you. I won't hide it. You're a Brahman, like god on earth. The sap of a certain magical plant was given to me by the kindness of god. It's an ointment for one's feet. Through its power, I move around, confident, faster than wind or mind.

We move as fast and as far
as the horses that pull the sun,
and we're never weary."

The Brahman, restless and eager,
folded his hands and said: "You're a great man.
Pardon my impudent words. How could I have known
your power? Be kind to me. I'm your pupil.
I wish to travel to the holy places.
Make it happen."

The siddha opened his basket of cane where he kept
his mercury *liṅga* and took out
an ivory casket.[14] He smeared a certain juice
on Pravara's feet without saying
a word.

The siddha left, and the Brahman
instantly took off, burning
with the wish to see the snow-capped peaks

of the Himalayas, the dark beckoning forests,
caves glittering with gold, and rushing rivers.

Hearing the birds say this, Jaimini asked: "What happened
next? This story of great piety is very exciting. Please have
the goodness to go on."

My king! Your fame, white as the spotless waves
of the Ganges, has washed away the blot on the moon.
You have unchallenged authority in every art.
You speak with the depth of the thousand-tongued first snake.

FAR FROM HOME

Listen, Krishnaraya, love god in human form,
ruling like Indra over the entire earth between
Sandal Mountain and Snow Mountain.
You're like Bhoja when you play with your poets,[15]
like a tree that grants all wishes
to the wise.

Those eminently intelligent birds went on telling the story
to Jaimini, as follows.

The Brahman went and saw Snow Mountain, its tall peaks
kissing the expanse of sky, with many rivers rushing

downward, rumbling like the beating of a drum,
on and on, while peacocks danced in time,
spreading their splendid tails,
and elephants roaming the slopes
shook the *sal* trees with their trunks.

He saw it, and waves of joy rushed through his mind.

The Brahman walked along a path
lined by jujube trees,
where Nara and Narayana had left their footprints,[16]
and as he walked, in front of him

bees were buzzing, drunk on waves of fragrance
from *kadamba* buds blossoming through the spray
of the Alaka River in spate,
and a gentle breeze carried
that sweet sound.

Elephants stretched their trunks to catch hold of tender
        leaf buds
on the *andugu* trees, and their tusks gleamed in the sun.
Tigers were snoring in the bushes while forest flies
pricked the edges of their lips.
Wild boars were digging up roots on the sand islands
in the mountain rivers.
Gayal, like big cattle, came jumping out of the wild shrubs.
Bears tore open honeycombs with their fearsome claws
and bees pouring out, flying through the air,
cast spots of shadow on the earth,

bathed in sunlight, here and there,
like white rice mingled with black sesame seeds.

The Brahman was looking,
his excitement rising. He was eager
to see it all—every cave hidden
in the forests that covered the slopes
of that mountain, leaving no gap.

The place where Sagara's great-grandson,
Bhagiratha, sat in penance until his thick long hair
turned to dreadlocks—
and where the river from the sky
came crashing down to earth, exposing the spine
of the ancient tortoise—
and where Parvati, the mountain's daughter,
setting aside her shyness, served her future husband
and suffered hardship—
the sad place where the prince of passion
was burnt to cinders by the fire
from Shiva's third eye—
and where even blameless fire
was consumed by desire for the beauty
of the Brahmans' wives,
where the reeds and grasses
gave birth to Kumara, general of the gods[17]—

the Brahman was overjoyed
to see it all.

"In every cycle, at the end of the world,
this earth is burnt to ash
and then again takes shape,
as beautiful as ever,
and everything grows back.
None of this would ever happen
without this mountain
to cool things down.

Here Shiva, lord of ghosts,
a snake stained yellow across his chest,
found a wife.[18] Here, in Sky River,
Indra discovered the joy of water games
while teaching his wife how to swim.
Here earth took the form of a cow, heavy with milk,
and nursed the hills, which burst into green.
Here Mena, swelling with pride among all the women
of the gods, learned how to wear the nine precious jewels.
Here all the gods found delicious taste and did away
with the boring blandness on their tongues
because this mountain provided whatever was needed
for their rites.

Not even God the creator
could do justice to the greatness
of this mountain! I'll come back tomorrow
to see more. Today
I have to go home. I can hear the sound
of snow melting on the sun-baked rocks, and that means
it's high noon."

He tried to turn back, but the water from melting snow
had washed the juice off his feet. The poor Brahman didn't
notice. Who can outdo fate?

Without that magical juice, his feet
couldn't move. He wanted to go home
in the worst way. A sudden grief
took hold. He thought to himself:
"God, you used that siddha
to bring me to this godforsaken place!

Where is my Arunaspada
and where is this Snow Mountain?
Why did I come here? Was I out of my mind?
I don't even know the way I took
to get here. How will I get back?

If I wanted to test the power
of that damned juice, I could have gone
to holy places like Maya,* Dvaraka,
Avanti, Kashi, Kurukshetra, Gaya,
or Prayaga. Why did I have to choose
a place infested by rhinoceroses, elephants,
wild boars, wild buffaloes, and tigers?
But then we're crazy. That's how Brahmans
who chant the Veda are made.

If my father doesn't see me
for even a minute, he hunts all over the village.

---

* Haridwar.

73

My mother won't even let me leave the house
after dark.
My loving wife, who is always in my heart—
she must be in agony.
And what about my students, always as close to me
as my shadow?
All of them must be worried.
Who's there to look after guests
or tend the fires?
Cruel fate—you've taken me away
from my daily rites and duties and cast me off
in this place at the end of the world where the sky
falls to earth.

Is there no kind soul somewhere nearby
who could take me home?"
He was drowning in a sea of sorrow
and terrified. He kept on walking
and saw before him

a wooded corner of a valley lined with red rock
as if the mountain had been cut straight from the top
all the way down by Indra's diamond weapon.
The Ganges was flowing there, and on the cool, sandy
          banks
of the river the forest was so thick that the rays of the sun
couldn't enter, and in that darkness areca and *ponna,*
orange, banana, and coconut trees were growing.
The calls of cuckoos, mynahs, parrots, peacocks,
bees, and herons were echoing off the moonstones,

and the whole valley was ringing with the music
of singers from heaven.[19]

Seeing all this, he thought, eager,
"Sages must be living here.
If I go there, they'll show me a way."
He calmed down just a little.

5.

Selections from *Poems from the Guru Granth Sahib*

by Guru Nanak

Translated from Panjabi by Nikky-Guninder Kaur Singh

Panjab—a region resounding with the songs of Bhagats and Sufis, lovers of god from various Indic and Islamic traditions—was the birthplace of Guru Nanak, founder of the Sikh religion, in 1469. He died there in 1539. His vast literary corpus—974 hymns recorded in the Guru Granth Sahib (GGS), the scripture of the Sikhs—embodies his pluralistic vision of the singular divine (*ikka*) in a multiethnic, multilinguistic, and multireligious world.

Eventually, Guru Nanak established a town named Kartarpur on the banks of the Ravi River, where he settled. The men and women who gathered there to hear and sing his sublime poetry and to practice the values of equality, civic action, and inclusivity formed the first Sikh community. He was fully conscious of the novelty of his message and practice and therefore sought to build an infrastructure that would provide momentum for later generations.[1] Although historical documentation on Guru Nanak is largely lacking, his life story is deeply imprinted in the collective memory of the Sikhs.[2]

Sikhs revere the Guru Granth Sahib—which translates literally as "the honored Guru in book form"—as the embodiment of their gurus. The sacred book constitutes the core of their ethics, philosophy, and aesthetics. It presides at all their ceremonies, rituals, and worship. The final canonical verseion of the GGS includes writings by several of Guru Nanak's nine successors.[3]

The compositions span five centuries and represent regions across the Indian subcontinent. Various authors exalt the divine One in a kaleidoscope of images, allusions, and symbols; they also offer compelling critiques of the ancient caste system, untouchability, religious divisions, and basic human degradation. The GGS serves as an important historical archive, bringing together a range of religions, cultures, ethnicities, languages, and musical measures.

Guru Nanak's language is archaic Panjabi that draws upon a variety of regional languages and local dialects. Besides Siraiki, the language of southwestern Panjab, and old Khari Boli, the language of the Delhi region and the basis of modern Hindi and Urdu, Guru Nanak abundantly utilizes vocabulary drawn from Persian, Sanskrit, and Arabic. The GGS has come down in a script named Gurmukhi, literally "from the Guru's mouth." Gurmukhi can be traced back to the Landa mercantile shorthand, also called Mahajani, that Guru Nanak used as a youth. His immediate successor developed and standardized the script.

His wide-ranging works use different meters, rhymes, stanzas, and compositional styles. His basic poetic form is the *saloku* (*śloka* in Sanskrit), a rhyming couplet with sixteen syllables in each line, sometimes printed as four half-lines of eight syllables each. Guru Nanak does not follow the syllabic pattern rigidly and creates subtle and powerful shifts by using parallelism between the halves of a line. *Salokus* combine into longer compositions such as *vārs,* popular Panjabi folk ballads depicting heroic events. Guru Nanak adapted the form's narrative style but transformed its historical battlefield setting into a metahistorical, spiritual sphere. Successor gurus adopted his model, and there are altogether twenty-two in the GGS. The *vārs* conclude with a rhyming *paurī* verse, an envoi.

In "Morning Hymn," Guru Nanak celebrates the singular reality and its qualities and names the formless all-inclusive being "truth" (*satu/sacu*)—an absolute expression of the unity shared across the celestial, terrestrial, and nether worlds. The thirty-eight stanzas of this hymn portray the singular being as an all-embracing *becoming* that flows in the cosmos and seeps into the human world of motions and emotions. Guru Nanak expresses his ontological, epistemological, aesthetic, ethical, and soteriological views through the five spheres: morality (*dharamu*), knowledge (*giānu*), beauty (*saramu*), action (*karamu*), and truth (*sacu*).

Guru Nanak identifies himself as a poet. His aesthetic consists of hearing, singing, and rejoicing in the infinite ensemble of vibrations: the individual (the heartbeat of every species), the social (every class, caste, ethnicity), and the ever-expanding multiverse. The divinely inspired Guru tried to awaken his followers and revitalize their senses, psyches, imaginations, and spirits through poetry. His literary genius lies in his ability to express profound metaphysical concepts in pithy and plain diction.

MORNING HYMN

There is only One. Truth by name.
    Creator Purakhu, without fear, without hate,
    timeless in form, unborn, self-existent,
    recognized by the guru's grace.

Recite:[4]
True in the beginning, true across the ages,
true in the now,
    Nanak: true forever.

One thought cannot think, nor can a million thoughts,
Silence cannot silence, nor can unbroken adoration.
The hunger of the hungry does not go away,
    not by the wealth of the whole world.
A thousand clever tricks can become a million,
    but not even one goes with us at the end.
How then to be truthful?
    How to break the wall of lies?
Follow the will, says Nanak, written down for us.[5]

By the will all forms are created,
    what the will is no one can say.
By that will all life is formed, all are made great.
The will determines the high and the low,
    the will writes out joy and suffering.[6]
The will blesses some, others wander endlessly.
All exist within the will, nothing stands apart.
Nanak: who knows the will won't say I or me.[7]

Those filled with might sing of its might,
those seeing its signs sing of its bounty,
the virtuous sing of its glory,
deep thinkers sing of its knowledge.
Some sing of the One who molds the body and turns it to
    dust,
some sing of its giving and taking life,
some sing of how far it seems in the distance,
some sing of how closely it watches all, ever present.
Stories upon stories, no end to the stories,
told and retold by millions and millions.
The giver gives, receivers tire of receiving,
age upon age they devour the gifts.
The leader leads by way of the will,
free from care, is ever joyful, says Nanak.

The true Sahib, true by name,[8]
    speaks the language of infinite love.
They speak and ask, "Give us, please give,"
    and the giver keeps giving.
What can we offer so we behold the divine court?
What words can we speak to be held dear?
In the timeless dawn praise the true name. Dwell on it.
Our actions give us this garment, the body.
    The gaze of love leads to the gate of liberation.
Nanak: know it for what it is, all this is truth itself.

The One can't be molded or made,[9]
pure, absolute, only itself.
Serve and be honored.

Nanak: sing of that treasure of virtues,
sing, listen, and hold love in your heart,
for sorrow is banished and joy enters.
Through the guru comes the numinous sound,[10]
    through the guru comes knowledge of the Vedas,
    through the guru the One is experienced in all.
The guru is Shiva, the guru is Vishnu, the guru is
    Brahma,[11]
    the guru is Parvati, Lakshmi, and Sarasvati.[12]
Were I to grasp it I'd still fail to explain
    the One beyond all telling.
The guru granted me one insight—
all living beings have the one giver,
    I must never forget.

I would bathe at a pilgrimage ford if it pleased the One,
    why bathe otherwise?
This entire span of creation I see
    couldn't exist without good deeds.
Hear a single teaching from the guru,
    and the mind shines with jewels, rubies, and pearls.
The guru gave me one insight—
all living beings have the one giver,
    I must never forget.

Were we to live through the four ages, or even ten times
    four,
were we known in the nine realms, hailed as leaders by all,
winning good name, glory, and fame across the world,

but were denied the gaze of love, we'd be cast out,
we'd be the lowest of worms, accused as the worst
    criminals.
Nanak: the One gives virtues to those who lack them, and
    to the virtuous gives even more.
That one of us could give virtue to the One is beyond
    thought.

Listening, we become like siddhas, naths, and *pīrs,*[13]
listening, we fathom the earth, the underworld, and skies,
listening, we know the nine continents, the many worlds
    and underworlds,
listening, death can't come near us.
Nanak: the devout enjoy bliss forever,
listening removes all suffering and evil.

Listening, we become like Shiva, Brahma, and Indra,
listening makes the corrupt open their mouths in praise,
listening reveals yoga discipline and the body's mysteries,
listening shines light on the shastras, smritis, and Vedas.
Nanak: the devout enjoy bliss forever,
listening removes all suffering and evil.

Listening leads to truth, contentment, knowledge,
listening bathes us in the sixty-eight sacred sites,
listening wins scholarly fame,
listening inspires serene focus.
Nanak: the devout enjoy bliss forever,
listening removes all suffering and evil.

Listening, we plumb the depths of virtues,
listening, we rise to the status of *shaikhs, pīrs,* and kings,
listening, the blind find their way,
listening, our hands touch the unfathomable.
Nanak: the devout enjoy bliss forever,
listening removes all suffering and evil.

No words can tell the state of embracing,[14]
try explaining it and you'll regret later.
No paper, no pen, no scribe can describe it,
philosophizing is no help to realize it.
So wondrous is the stainless name,
only those who embrace it in their mind know it.

Embracing
	our mind and intellect awaken,
embracing
	we learn of all the worlds,
embracing
	our face is safe from blows,
embracing
	we part company with death.
So wondrous is the stainless name,
only those who embrace it in their mind know it.

Embracing
	we walk on a clear path,
embracing
	we advance in honor and glory,

embracing
    we don't stray down lanes and byways,
embracing
    we bond with righteousness.
So wondrous is the stainless name,
only those who embrace it in their mind know it.

Embracing
    we find the door to liberation,
embracing
    we liberate our family too,
embracing
    we swim and carry the guru's learners across,
embracing, says Nanak,
    we need not beg around.
So wondrous is the stainless name,
only those who embrace it in their mind know it.

The five win approval, the five are the leaders,[15]
they receive honors at court,
shine splendidly at the royal gates,
attend to the only guru.
However much we speak or think,
the creator's doings are beyond calculation.
The bull that bears the earth is righteousness, child of
    compassion,
its rope is contentment holding the earth in balance.
We will live truthfully once we realize
how heavy a weight the bull bears,

for there is not one earth but many more, above and
    beyond—
who stands beneath supporting them all?
The names of living beings, their varieties and colors,
were all written in a single pen stroke.
Were one to write this writ,
what endless writ it would be.
What power, beauty of form,
how great a gift—how to assess it?
This wide expanse from a single command,
from it a million rivers flew forth.
How to fathom or express this creative power?
I cannot offer myself to you even once,
only that which pleases you is good.
You are forever constant, formless One.

Countless are the ways of meditation,
    countless the avenues of love,
countless the ways of worship,
    countless the prayers and penances.
Countless texts and Vedic reciters,
countless yogis who turn from the world.
Countless the devout reflecting on virtue and knowledge,
countless the pious and their patrons,
countless warriors who face iron,
countless sages sunk in silent trance—
Who can express or fathom the creative power?
I cannot offer myself to you even once,
only that which pleases you is good.
You are forever constant, formless One.

Countless fools lost in pitch darkness,
countless thieves living off others,
countless tyrants bullying their way to immortality,
countless cut-throats with blood on their hands,
countless evil misdeeds trailing behind them,
countless liars spinning their lies,
countless perverts devouring filth,
countless slanderers bent by their burden.
Lowly Nanak thinks and says:
I cannot offer myself to you even once,
only that which pleases you is good.
You are forever constant, formless One.

Countless are your names, countless your places,
unreachable and unfathomable your countless spheres.
Even saying "countless" is a weight on our heads.
Yet by words we name, by words we acclaim,
by words we know and sing and praise.
By words we write, speak, and perform,
in words actions are written on our forehead,
        our blessed union proclaimed.[16]
Yet on the writer's forehead nothing is written,
as the One orders, so each of us receives.
As wide creation is, so is the name—
there is no place without it.
Who can express this creative power?
I cannot offer myself to you even once,
only that which pleases you is good.
You are forever constant, formless One.

Dirty hands feet skin body
are washed clean with water.[17]
Pee-stained clothes
are washed with soap too.
A mind polluted by evil
is cleansed by the color of the name.
Good and evil are not mere words,
the actions we do, get written and go with us:
we reap but what we sow,
Nanak: by the will we come and go.

Pilgrimage, austerity, mercy, gifts, charity—
their merit is barely worth a sesame seed.
By listening, embracing, and evoking love,
we scrub ourselves clean
    at the name's ford within.
Every virtue rests in you, in me I have none,
without doing good deeds devotion is impossible.
We praise you—our wealth, sacred verse, creator god,[18]
you are true, you are beauty, you are joy forever.
What was the time, the hour?
    What was the date, the day?
What was the season, the month,
    when creation took its form?
If pandits knew the time, it would be written in the
    Puranas,
if *qazis* knew the hour, it would be written in the Qur'an,
no yogi knows the date or day, no one knows the month or
    season,
only the creator knows who designed this creation.

How can I speak of the One?
>How can I praise?
>How can I describe?
>How can I know?
Nanak: how many speak of the One, each smarter than the
>other.
Great is the Sahib, great its name,
>all that happens is its doing.
Nanak: those who think they know
>are not adorned in the hereafter.

Worlds below worlds, million worlds above worlds.
Tired of seeking their limits, the Vedas say it's all one
>thing,
the Kateb say eighteen thousand,
>but really it is one reality.
If it could be written it would have been written,
>but writing vanishes.
Nanak: praise the great One
>who alone knows itself.

Praisers praise, but do not know your vastness
like rivers and streams flow to the ocean
>unaware of its expanse.
Emperors and sultans rule over kingdoms vast as oceans,
>own wealth piled high as mountains,
yet none can match an ant whose mind does not forget.

Infinite is the One's glory and infinite the song of praise,
infinite the deeds and infinite the gifts,

infinite is the seeing, infinite the listening,
and infinite the workings of its mind.
Infinite are the created forms,
infinite the limits here and beyond.
How many cry, yearning to learn these limits?
Even their end is not to be found,
the end eludes us all,
the more it's expressed, the farther it extends.
Our Sahib is great, high its status,
and higher still its name.
Only were we ever to reach that height,
would we know the highest One.
Its greatness, it alone knows.
Nanak: the glance of love is its gift.

Great is your favor, how can one write about it?
Great the giver, with no trace of greed.
So many mighty heroes beg you
so many more than we can know.
So many waste themselves in vicious acts,
so many take and take yet deny their giver,
so many fools just eat and eat,
so many are devoured by pain and hunger, but
these too are your gifts, our giver.
Your will frees us from bondage,
no one else here has a say,
the fool who dares speak up
gets so many slaps on his face.
You alone know, you alone give,
how few though acknowledge this.

The person gifted to praise and adore,
Says Nanak, is truly the emperor of emperors.

Priceless are your virtues, priceless how they're traded,
priceless are their dealers, priceless the treasures in store,
priceless the customers, priceless what they take away,
priceless is love, priceless those immersed in it,
priceless is the law and priceless the court.
Priceless are the scales, priceless the weights,
priceless is bounty, priceless its sign,
priceless is the action, priceless the command.
How priceless the priceless One is, no one can say,
those who try are rapt in silence.
Vedas and Puranas say,
scholars say in their texts and discourses,
Brahmas say, Indras say,
gopīs and Govindas say,
Shivas say, siddhas say,
countless buddhas say,
demons say, gods say,
divine folks, silent sages, and the devout say.
How many speak and begin to speak,
how many have spoken and gone as they spoke.
Were their number doubled again,
no one still could say the slightest bit.
That One is as great as it chooses to be,
Nanak: only the true One knows itself.
The babbler who presumes to speak
is written down as the fool of fools.

What sort of gate is it, what house
    where you sit caring for all?[19]
So many instruments and melodies,
    so many musicians who praise you,
countless ragas and their fairies, we say,[20]
    and so many singers to sing to you.
To you sing wind, water, and fire,
    the king of righteousness sings at your door.[21]
To you sing Chitra and Gupta,[22]
    recording actions for the judge to decide.
To you sing Shiva, Brahma, and the goddess
    whose splendor you forever adorn.
To you sing Indras upon Indras
    sitting among gods at the gate.[23]
To you sing siddhas in meditation,
    to you sing sages in contemplation.
To you sing ascetics, the true, the contented,
    to you sing invincible heroes.
To you sing pandits and the best of seers
    reading the Vedas in every age.
To you sing beautiful women who enchant the mind
    in heaven, on earth, and in the netherworlds.
To you sing the jewels that you created
    along with the sixty-eight sacred sites.
To you sing heroes and mighty warriors,
    to you sing the four sources of life.[24]
To you sing continents, constellations, and universes—
    all created and sustained by you.
They sing to you, your devotees
    who please you and revel in your love.

How many others sing to you I can't imagine,
    Nanak, how can I think of them?
That One, the ever-true Sahib
    who is true, and whose name is true,
is and ever will be;
    never will the creator of the creation not be.
In many colors and many varied forms,
    the One who created illusion
watches everything it created.
    All this is the One's greatness.
Whatever the One desires comes to pass,
    no one can challenge its commands.
Nanak: all abide by the will
    of the emperor of emperors.

Contentment your yogic earrings, beauty your begging
    pouch,[25]
    smear yourself with the ashes of contemplation;
death shall be the cloak for your virgin body,
    and yoga and belief, the staff you lean on;
the Mother's sect accepts all people.[26]
    Conquer the mind to conquer the world.
All praise, all praise to the One—
timeless, pure, with no beginning or end,
    ever the same form, age to age.

With knowledge the banquet, and compassion the
    treasurer,[27]
    hear the sacred music sound in every heart.

The One is the master with all under its sway,
 why go for feats and miracles that lead you astray?
The One sets up our meeting, sets up our parting,
 we get what is written for us.
All praise, all praise to the One—
timeless, pure, with no beginning or end,
 ever the same form, age to age.

One mother, created in mystical union,
 three, her approved disciples:
creator, treasurer, and holder of court.
Everything works as the One decrees,
 all are under its command.
The One sees us all, yet marvel of marvels,
 none of us can see that One at all.
All praise, all praise to the One—
timeless, pure, with no beginning or end,
 ever the same form, age to age.

Its seat and its treasury are in every world.
Whatever is was placed there once for all time.
Ever creating, the creator beholds all it creates.
Nanak, the works of the true one are true forever.
All praise, all praise to the One—
timeless, pure, with no beginning no end,
 ever the same form, age to age.

If this one tongue became a hundred thousand,
 and each then became twenty times more,

a hundred thousand times over they'd speak of
    the one name of Jagdish,* who owns the world.
This is the way to climb the stairs to become one with the
    One.[28]
Hearing these sky-high stories,
    even insects are spurred to imitate.
Nanak: the One is attained by the gaze of love,
    not by the boasting of the false.

It's not for us to speak or stay silent,
it's not for us to ask or give,
it's not for us to live or die,
it's not for us to gain riches that rattle the mind.
It's not for us to have consciousness, knowledge, or
    reflection,
it's not for us to escape the world-wheel,
the One whose hand holds power watches over us all.
Nanak: no one is too high or too low.

Nights and seasons, dates and days,
air, water, fire, and netherworlds,
in their middle is the earth, the place of righteous action.
In its midst, lifestyles and beings of every hue,
with endless names and countless forms.
You reflect on every action,
you are true, truly just your court,
there the accepted five are adorned,[29]

----

* "Master of the world," a term for the divine.

95

their actions marked with the gaze of love.
The raw and the ripened are judged over there,[30]
Nanak: we come to know this when we reach.

Such is the order of the realm of duty,[31]
now tell us about the actions for the realm of knowledge.[32]
So many airs, waters, and fires,
    so many Krishnas and Shivas,
so many Brahmas fashioned in such variety of
    forms, colors, and guises.
So many earths and mountains to live and act in,
    so many Dhruvas to give instructions,[33]
so many Indras, moons, and suns,
    so many continents and universes,
so many siddhas, buddhas, naths,
    so many kinds of goddesses.
So many gods, demons, and sages,
    so many jewels and oceans,
so many species, so many languages,
    so many rulers and kings.
So many mystics, so many devotees,
    Nanak: there's just no end to their end.

In the realm of knowledge,
    knowledge blazes forth.
Here is numinous sound, feasting, cheering, and joy.
Now the realm of beauty is beauty itself,[34]
here shapes are inimitably designed.
Words fail description,

those who try, regret later.
Here consciousness, wisdom, mind, and discernment are
    sharpened,[35]
awareness whetted like the gods' and siddhas'.

The realm of action speaks of force.[36]
Here is the One, no other.
Here live heroes and mighty warriors,
filled with the strength of Ram.
Here are Sitas upon Sitas of great fame,[37]
their beauty beyond words.
They do not die, are not beguiled
for Ram is in their mind.
Here live devotees from many worlds
blissfully happy, for the true One beats in their heart.
In the realm of truth lives the formless One,[38]
ever creating,
    the One beholds with the gaze of blissful love.
Here are continents, constellations, universes
whose limits cannot be told.
Here are living beings of manifold forms,
all acting according to the will.
The One watches, rejoices, and reflects on its creation.
Nanak: to describe this is as hard as iron.

Discipline the smithy, patience the goldsmith,[39]
wisdom the anvil, knowledge the hammer,
with awe the bellows, stoke the fire within.[40]
Ambrosia pours out in the vat of love,[41]

the sacred word is cast in the true mint
—this is the action of those blessed by the gaze of love.
Nanak: those on whom the gaze falls are blissful and free.

Epilogue
Air is our guru, water our father,
    the great earth our mother,
day and night, our female and male nurses
    in whose lap the whole world plays.[42]
Good and bad, our actions are judged
    in the presence of righteousness,
it is they who take us near or far.
Those remembering the name,
    depart honored for their labor.
Nanak: their faces shine, and they carry with them
    many more to liberation.

6.

Selections from *Sur's Ocean*

by Surdas

Translated from Hindi
by John Stratton Hawley

Surdas—the exemplary poet of Krishna whose name means literally "servant (*dās*) of the sun (*sūr*)"—is considered the epitome of poetic artistry in Braj Bhasha, one of the major literary strands of Hindi. The language is deeply associated with Braj, the region that stretches south from Delhi along the River Yamuna where the god Krishna is remembered as having spent his boyhood. Sur's primary narrative métier was the world of Krishna—from his childhood and amorous youth through to his role in the epic Mahabharata.

Any attempt to assign birth and death dates to Surdas is doomed to fail. Biographically speaking, all we can know is that this great poet lived somewhere in north India in the sixteenth century. The authorial identity called Surdas actually describes a literary tradition that was many decades, even centuries, in the making.

The oldest extant dated manuscript that contains poems attributed to Sur was written in Fatehpur in the year 1582. It comprises 239 poems attributed to Sur, along with a number credited to other poets.[1] Later collections assume oceanic dimensions appropriate to the designation *Sur's Ocean* (*Sūrsāgar*); by the nine-

99

teenth century, there was a manuscript containing almost ten thousand poems.[2]

Who then "composed" this ocean? Neither the traditional response of a single individual nor the notion of collective authorship is completely satisfactory.[3]

Although we can grant that the *Sūrsāgar* is not a static thing produced by a single poet, but rather a "Sur tradition," this does not explain how the name Surdas came to be associated with a particular poetical style and expertise.[4] For this reason, we must retain a sense of a single excellent poet standing at the headwaters of the Sur tradition.

Many poems in *Sur's Ocean* focus on the Krishna narrative. Among them are the endless permutations on the beauties and frustrations of love, adumbrated in poems that would have been as successful in a court, home, or bazaar as in a temple. It is perhaps significant that Radha is named far less frequently in Surdas's poems than one might expect. If his heroine was invariably Radha, as modern scholars tend to assume, Surdas certainly does not always say so. Typically he leaves her unnamed, giving us only the female lover par excellence; and Krishna, by implication, often emerges in an amorous role rather than a specifically religious one. Indeed, the distinction between secular and religious—or court and temple—can be hard to make, and that is true in many corners of Braj Bhasha literature.[5] In this regard, as in others, then, Sur remains patron saint of Braj Basha literature as a whole.

Poetry can be the means of envisioning all that is beautiful—the ideal—but it is also a salve for our wounds, the sense we've been forgotten. In *Sur's Ocean*, we have both. And the greatness of the poet is that we do.

THE PANGS AND POLITICS OF LOVE

1

Separation, Lord of Braj, makes us women despair.
Lord, oh lord, don't make us lordless orphans—
that is our cry as we stretch forth our arms,
for the love of Hari and our youthful pride
have made us unable to bridle our tongues.
What's to be done? What fault there is, is ours.
Murari is scarcely to blame.
The lanes, the bathing places, mountains and their caves—
our eyes have searched and dimmed,
succumbed to floods of tears.
Surdas says, Out of arrogance of body
our everything is stolen away.

2

The water tumbles, tumbles down the face[6]
as if before one's eyes one saw the Ganges fall
on the head of Shiva, who then showers the earth.
That fearsome lion's waist, the beggar's tangled hair—
yet still, a pillar of beauty:
A necklace of pearls decorates breasts
held tight by a slender bodice,
and curls scattered about the face radiate
an amazing cloud of bees.
Surdas says, In the Mountain Lifter's presence,
any shred of pretense disappears.

3

Nanda's Joy is playing in the waters of the Jamuna:
on all four sides, a lovely band of cowherd girls,
and in the center, the Destroyer of Disaster.[7]
Their hands, how they sparkle as they splash one another;
their arms too, as the sandal paste dissolves.
It's as if the girls were worshiping the lord of snakes
by daubing vermilion on his limbs.
Tiny beads of water form on the tips of his hair,
thick with curls, and set loose languid drops
as if joyful bees had gathered lotus pollen—
so much that it sprays in little volleys from their mouths.
Like a hunter snaring birds, his embraces lure the girls
into faraway fathomless waters,
and sages sing the virtues of the husband of Shri,
the master of Surdas, with their verse.

4

When Radha takes the water's child in her hand,[8]
a deep red beauty springs into being
and all the ganders flee.
Cakors come and gather at that face
but hesitate and stand some distance away.
Then Brishabhanu's daughter gives a smile
and the two begin to quarrel:
the sun and the moon, set in a single chariot,
face each other stubbornly,
but Surdas's lord relaxes in the groves
and is filled with bounding joy.

5

The beauty of Lord Hari's eyes:
when I think of it in my mind, they make it seem
the lotus is worshiping the sun.
As if wagtails' darting motions were for naught,
as if deer should hide in the forest,
and fish should hide in the water—
something like this is what bad poets say
in searching for metaphors.
For those eyes are only like those eyes, my friend,
and I'm lost: nothing else sheds light.
Every simile I've found, says Sur,
is just another offering for the fire.

6

Why did we store away the honey of those lips,
gather it and hoard it—foolish us!—like bees
and never allow ourselves a taste?
Why did we suffer the frigid waters of the Jamuna,
daily mounting our pitiful petitions,
praying Uma's lord, Shiva, to send us a bridegroom
and satisfy the longings of our hearts?
Now it's Murali who drinks that nectar,
pushing everyone else aside.
Listen, Sur, she's absconded with him fearlessly
and kicked the cow dust in our eyes.

7

Murali has become Mohini.[9]
You know what she did to the gods

and antigods: now she's done it again.
They churned the milk sea; we, a sea of vows,
and obtained a new immortal nectar:
an oceanic liquid, held in Hari's lunar face,
that she stealthily snatches away
and quaffs down, making us drink octaves of sound
that pour from her victory tour.
One single vessel—then it held elixir,
but now, says Sur, intoxicating liquor.

8

Why do you cowherd women slander me so?
You ought to ask Shyam how much pain it took,
how much pain to earn his love.
From the moment I was born, I've set aside the world—
my town, my skills, my home:
I practiced the penance of standing on one foot
through winter, summer, and throughout the rains;
I did without roots and branches and leaves.
With worries my body was parched and dried,
then pierced by that fiery rod: those holes!
Dreadful though it was, I never cringed.
So why keep saying, "She's just some bamboo stick,"
murmuring with rage?
Do what it takes to please Surdas's lord
and you too can take the liquid from his lips.

9

This is how things have settled in my mind:
if I left Gopal and turned my thoughts to someone else,

I'd be my mother's disgrace.
What would I gain by amassing a heap of glass
and throwing away a precious jewel?
Is it better to have a whole Mount Meru of poison
than a drop of the liquid that gives life?
My mind and words and acts—purified, all three:
Shyam is the master of my then and yet to be.
Surdas's lord, for the sake of singing your praise
I've even given up my caste.[10]

10

"Kanh, you've been badgering me since dawn.
Why single me out for your stubbornness—
raising a ruckus in broad daylight,
blocking off the path?
Well, you can't have a thing until the first sale,
or else you might as well take it all.
Day after day I go to Mathura to sell:
Who said you could take a share?
Show me the paper where it's written!
First you kiss my face, then embrace my breast,
and after that you're so intent
you spill everything else."
Surdas says, The milkmaid's love began to show.
Even though he'd let her go,
she wouldn't budge from the road.

11

"Why not simply take that 'gift' of yours?
Dispense with any more of this absurd behavior,

and Nanda's son, drop that threatening stick.
You've pounced on me and grabbed my sari,
blocked the road so as not to let me pass,
and all the while there's something you're not saying.
What's made you act this way?"
"Today I'm not letting you go home, cowherd girl.
I've had this in mind for a very long time."
Thus the lord of Surdas took her to his bower
and gave a gift of nail marks to her breast.

12

Sold for a smile on his face!
I've fallen into a single, simple habit:
I roam day and night in someone else's power.
My eyes, seeing him, have made themselves his envoys,
and my mind dissolves in him like water in milk
while Passion's lord* has seized my modesty from its fort
and offered it to Hari as tribute.
Listen, my reason is enslaved to handsome Shyam—
this it knows, friend, for all time.
Everything he tells me to do, I do.
I've taken his command on my brow.
No more body vanity, fancies, frenzies,
no more husband or family or friends—
he's an ocean, says Sur, and I'm a brimming stream
who's lost her last yearning drop to the sea.

---

* Kama, husband of "Passion," or Rati.

13

What can anyone do to me?
The world can deride me all it likes,
but I'll never swerve from my resolve.
Let them huddle and talk behind my back,
let them scream it out before my face—
I don't care. I'm not so weak of brain
that I'd turn away from Hari and go off with someone else.
From here on out my life is as it is:
I've settled myself in Shyam's dark home,
And Sur, my heart is dyed a color so deep
that it will never turn white again.

14

Living in a single town as we do,
how can I hold myself back?
Try though I may, my eyes, like bees,
 refuse to accept constraint.
On this very road he comes to herd his cows
as I set out to sell my curds,
and my body hairs bristle, my voice begins to choke,
I can't contain my excitement.
Once he's out of sight, an instant seems an era
as I burn in the fire of separation.
How many days can I keep this up, says Surdas,
and keep to the straight and narrow path?

15

Even then he wouldn't let go of the curd,
grasped it as if it held the four fruits of life[11]

until the Enemy of Night[12]
turned to a deer-faced new moon:
relishing the pleasures of ambrosial words,
he stuck to his stubborn, cajoling debate.
The lotuses of night began to bloom
and I wilted as the horses of the sun sank to earth;
I watched as he, knowing it was night,
took on a lunar form: adolescent, newfound youth.
The lord of Surdas: why has he left me now—
now that he's claimed my heart?

16

Radha, how you've burst into bloom!
The fathomless love you exude tells a tale
of Madhav's tight embrace.
Madan's arrows strain their bows, your brows,
to triangles half expanded;
with winsome looks and twisted glances they tap
a rhythm that forces Love himself to dance.
The experience that drew Shuk, Sanak, and the sages,
the object of Shiva's daily regimen—
that's the experience Sur's lord has given you,
the prayer even Shri does not attain.

17

Radha, how fine your face:
when you appear, cast your glance here and there,
it makes the lord of the night* turn pale.

* The moon.

You pull back your bow, those fully arched eyebrows,
and aim your sandalwood brow-mark arrow
such that it seems the hunter, Passion's lord,
has crouched behind your garments and veil.
You walk with the stride of an elephant in rut—
I swear it, I won't be moved.
In varied and manifold ways you've seduced
the heart of Sur's master,
Hari, whom you love.

18

He's opened wide his lotus-petal eyes
and the fascinating glances that emanate there
send secret, coded messages, friend.
His face is the lotus, and his curls gather around
like honey-drinking bees in search of honey.
His *tilak* mark is shaped like a youthful moon
and he speaks as if to laugh—
in a bewitching, honeyed tongue.
King Kama's land is an intoxicating place—
strength of mind cannot dwell there,
nor peace of heart.
Surdas's lord sends that king out day by day,
a messenger to bring his women's character
to the test.

19

I've found something the creator failed to do.
I looked at Govind today—I looked and then
I knew what was wrong, and lamented.[13]

He had dressed my frame in a dazzling way,
he'd given brilliance to my intellect, and yet
he neglected to give eyes to each tiny body hair,
and to that extent he failed in his art.
What am I to do? These poor strained eyes
are overwhelmed each instant, and overflow their lids.
How, says Sur, can Mount Meru be fit
into this worn-out little cup of a brain?

20

Beautiful glances: their restless, constant motion
cannot be described—it fascinates the mind—
generating something like a vortex.
He plays on Murali and sings, sweet as honey,
fingers glide and earrings sway,
and all this loveliness is gathered and reflected
in the sapphire mirror of the cheeks.
Curling locks of hair are like swarms of honeybees
drawn by the power of great fragrance.
Sur says: fine eyebrows, nose, glinting teeth—
to set the mind on these is a love beyond all price.

21

At the sight of Hari's face, my eyes lose their way:
they're love-struck bees who are mired in the mud
beneath a charming lotus, powerless then to fly.
His crocodile earrings on the banks of his cheeks
seem suns emerging from the night,
and his agile eyebrows move with such deftness
that wagtails and fish, at the sight, are moved to shame.

His lips are red flags and his diamond teeth, dewdrops
resembling a moon among clouds,
while his tangled locks of hair swarm like bees
who have finally reached the nectar they seek.
A *tilak* marks his forehead, pearls are at his neck,
and his other adornments are studded with jewels.
Surdas says, The yellow of his garment
and the darkness of Shyam—how can that fineness
fashion itself into words?

22

"Oh, those eyes' beguiling ways!—
strong enough, it seems, to surpass by far
the orbit of autumn lotuses.
Every quality and species has been vanquished—
indīvar, rājīv, kuśeśay*—
in an epic contest of happy, loving moods
that the eyes have won by blooming day and night."
Wagtails, fish, deer—when she considers
such metaphors as these, she despairs:
"Charming to behold,"
"Quick their darting looks"—
No. No thought fits.
"Let the eyelids drop for a moment's blink
and an instant passes like an age...."
So does Radha, taster of Sur's lord's moods,
rail at his eyes' propensity to close.

* Blue lotuses.

23

Coming to know the Dark One—to what end?
One minute this beauty; the next, that charm—
if you do fall in love, beware!
Your eyes may behold him constantly, night and day,
you may marshal your thoughts, your brains, your mind,
yet not for a single second will your heart attain
the boundary of his brilliance.
Even when he's present and you can touch him, to test,
you'll never fathom that mine of every bliss.
What is it, friend? Separation? Union? Both?
Is it joy or sorrow? Detriment or gain?
You can't douse a fire, says Sur, by pouring on ghee,
and that's what it's like with his lovely eyes:
on the one hand there's brilliance;
on the other, yet more charm;
and neither keeps to its side of the line.

24

What am I to do? I can't seem to have
a clear view of Hari's handsome form—
and that, though I stay with him night and day
and never blink an eye.
I chase after him as if bound to his sight
like a kite tied to a string,
But when I draw near, my own reflection
confounds me: it interferes.
I strain to see him all, head to toe,
the image that so satisfies the mind,
but somehow—how?—each and every part of him

becomes infused with *my* charms.
This body of mine has become my greatest foe:
though I'd hide it, it's not hidden.
No, it makes *him* hide, and the liquid
of my unabated love, says Surdas,
mounts inside—a tide.

25

My drive to see Hari has died,
flown off to the winds, gone wandering with my eyes,
like the cotton that explodes from the swallow-wort pod.
Is he saying something? I answer something else.
Hairs erect, drops of sweat drip with the labor of love.
Where has it come from—I just don't know—
this image that has grown up in my mind?
For a lonely woman like me, the pain of not seeing
is such feverish heat that any touch is hard to bear.
I'm wilted, says Sur, like a little sprout of grain,
as a root would wither without rain.

26

Ever since the day the Dark One appeared
and I was filled with love's nectar for that lad,
the cowherd with the beguiling form—
ever since that day these eyes have forgotten
all other joys and pains:
they've settled over there on the basis of a smile,
and busied themselves setting up house.
Body, mind, and intellect were sent to intercede,
but they've stubbornly persisted, night and day:

the more these emissaries asked them to return,
the more they were determined to stay,
so the envoys tired of all this thinking and explaining
and moved farther and farther away.
How can I describe, says Sur, the wealth these eyes survey?
So much, they never blink. Their gaze never strays.

27

What in the world has Hari done to me, my friend?
My mind understands, but my mouth can't find the words:
my eyes must have drunk some kind of potion, friend.
I was standing there, alone in my courtyard,
when suddenly he appeared, my friend.
I looked at him and found my faculties gone:
my mind had exchanged them all for him, my friend.
From excess of happiness, a pain I cannot bear,
burning, burning my heart cool, my friend.
Sur says, Every joy has come into my breast—
I can't find any other way to say it, my friend.

28

Nanda's darling has made off with my mind.
Early in the morning I was threading a string of pearls
when he tossed a pebble my way, my friend.
His sidelong glances and the charming way he moves
make Nanda's lad a connoisseurs' best jewel.
Who could keep her mind in tow, I'd like to know,
on hearing Murali's tasteful, honeyed sound?
Govind's face, which is the moon, has made
my eyes, which are *cakor* birds, burn,

and so, to win a meeting with Surdas's lord
I've sold my coconut breasts for a pittance—
sold them for nothing at all.[14]

29

Many the ways I've tried to reason with my mind,
but somehow it's so mired in the juice of endless love
that now it can no longer emerge.
The secrets of these eyes and the beauty they store
have worked their way inside my heart
and made it sleep complacently
while they escaped back to him.
Fearlessly it's jettisoned modesty and family,
doing only what it itself desires:
like an owl dazzled by a brilliant light,
it's gotten itself stubbornly entrapped.
He may be far away, he may be deep in the woods,
but it hurries to lose itself in his power.
Listen, Surij, what an upside-down affair:
Kama, from his coma, revived!

30

So you think this is like stealing butter!
When I'd recognize your face back then, I'd be glad,
I'd let you go. After all, the loss was small.
In those days I was just a simple girl,
so innocent I thought you were just a little boy.
You were the son of the greatest man in Braj,
and I didn't want butter to blacken the family name.
Now you've grown—to a deft and budding youth,

and I've grown too, wise in worldly ways.
So where do you think you're going,
wrenching away your arm
after stealing all the treasures of my soul?
Head to toe, you're a heart thief—every part.
I've found you out: why try to squirm away?
Here's something strange, says Sur, upside down:
you've gone and robbed my all,
but still I trail around in your thrall.

31

"How great your power! Oh I know, Yadav King:*
You've taken those arms and snapped yourself away
from a powerless woman like me!
They say you're clever in every way
and versed in every technique,
but I'll only believe it when you can take a step
that takes you from my heart."
The master of Surdas, husband of Shri,
feels what is felt inside.
He couldn't stand such love:
he turned back, smiled,
and folded her in an embrace.

32

Shyam, just drop that look you have
and wipe away that grin:
one little dose of your easy ways—theirs—

————

* Krishna.

and I've lost everything.
Triumph and Victory: Destiny has ordained
that the two of them behave exactly as they please:[15]
all they have to do is scan the scene before them,
and suddenly it's all within their power.
Then there's me. How can I describe the way
I've served as traitor to myself?
Whatever wealth I'd squirreled away in my little purse—
I've squandered, says Sur. I went berserk.

33

The heroine

"Friends, unite, find something that can be done!
The killer god[*] has come at me, a love-forlorn woman,
brandishing flowerbuds of desire;
the offering eater[†] has raised his banner,
and the wind blows from Hari's[‡] domain.
He who bears the son of the foe of the best-bowed one[§]
shouts out, shouts out its joyful song;
and as the son of the son of the waters[**] reels in circles,
I find there is nothing to be done.
Bring me now the beloved of my soul,
the one who made his friend bear Victory's[††] name."

———

* Mar, or Kama.
† Agni, fire.
‡ Here Indra, not Krishna or Vishnu.
§ Kama.
** The moon, whose son is intelligence.
†† Arjuna, whose friend is Krishna.

117

Her friend
"Consider the season. Cast aside your pride.[16]
Why not let it float off where it will?
Let yourself dwell in the shelter of Sur's lord,
who is monarch of all three worlds."

34

From seeing the Dark One, it seems I cannot see.
What am I to do? My eyes are battle-weary.
They've not blinked once—passed the night awake.
On this side of the fray, a charm Kama loves to see;
on that side, a radiance untraceable, unreached.
Like Arjun and Karna, these two have grown to be rivals,[17]
and neither will consider retreat—never!
I am poised for battle, in finery arrayed,
and he is opposed, his limbs like glistening mail.
My eyes, says Sur, are so filled with pride
that they'll only take the pleasure
of the Dark One as their prize.

35

To see it, it seems two egos arrayed:
on that side Hari's handsomeness, on this side my eyes—
both of them forces unyielding in war.
His charm and visage are great joys to the god of love,
and on this side they blend into one.
On that side his many different kinds of adornments
seem bows that are variously slung across his frame.
On this side a wrathless passion for him
showers quiverfuls of arrows with each blink of the eye.

On that side, in silent pain, his hairs stand on end
like arrows moving over every limb.
There, beauty incarnate; and love for Sur's lord here:
both gain in force with every passing moment
as if two vast oceans were filled with deathless nectar
and so greatly wished to meet, they overflowed.

36

Radha entwines herself limb for limb with Shyam.
Krishna, a black *tamāl* tree with tremulous branches—
she drapes herself around him like a girdle, a garland.
Mountain Lifter, now he holds the finest of mountains;
leader among lovers, he's won the battle of love.
Sur says, these two—both of them are warriors.
What enemy of love could intervene?

37

This friend of yours, lotuslike: where has she been
    hiding?[18]
This one—until just now I've never seen her.
Where did she come from today?
Robbing every virtue, the splendor of all three worlds,
the creator has fashioned a single being: you.
So where did you travel—to what city, tell me, Radha—
to find another cache of such unbearably fine form?
Searching my faculties, I've tried to imagine
how any other body could rival yours in beauty
for it's Brishabhanu's daughter—the one here before us—
who brings her companions every joy.
The lord of Sur has thrilled to your refinements,

observing the excellence of your eyes,
and I have marked it, so go to your forest bower
and abandon all this cleverness of mind.

38

My eyes, once they looked, could never turn away.
Greedy for the juice cupped in Hari's lotus mouth,
like honeybees they sank into drunkenness for honey.
They languished, my friend, behind bars—eyelid spears.
Day and night they stubbornly persevered,
but they were victims of deception, duped by a black snake
that sheds its slough like a bodice,
making them float, it seems, down love-swollen rivers
that course through mountain canyons—
cascades of sweat—
until every single drop was merged with Sur's lord.
I wonder where they'll ever come ashore.

39

My eyes have fallen into evil ways:
only if I focus on Hari's store of beauties
do they give me any satisfaction.
They're vultures, my friend. There's no way to snare them.
They've left behind every ounce of shame
as they gaze with lust at the moon of his lustrous face
like adoring *cakor* birds,
utterly unmoored, washed away in tears,
unable to live if that vision disappears.
What could I do? I gathered them up myself
and surrendered them, Sur, to Shyam's hands.

7.

Selections from
The Epic of Ram

by Tulsidas

Translated from Hindi
by Philip Lutgendorf

A poet of extraordinary versatility and vision, Tulsidas is celebrated as the author of a dozen works, most of which are dedicated to Ram. There are few details of his biography that have not been contested, beginning with his date of birth (variously posited as 1497, 1526, and 1543—the last being favored by the majority of modern scholars); a death date of 1623 is widely accepted. Some of his works hint at autobiographical details, and three include dates of composition, indicating that he was active during the reigns of the Mughal emperors Akbar and Jahangir. There is evidence that he spent a good part of his life in Banaras, regularly participated in the public performance of devotional texts, including his own, and was supported in part by the offerings of appreciative listeners.

His name means "servant of tulsi," referring to the "holy basil" plant considered especially pleasing to Vishnu, and thus signals the poet's likely initiation into a Vaishnava religious order or guru-lineage, *-dās* being a common suffix for initiatory names in several orders. The poet himself often shortens this name to "Tulsi" in his poetic "signature" (*chāp* or *bhaṇitā*).

The Epic of Ram (*Rāmcaritmānas;* literally, "Divine Lake of Ram's Deeds"), composed in Hindi by Tulsidas in 1574, is among the most beloved and revered works of Indian literature.[1] An epic poem composed in Hindi in the late sixteenth century, the *Mānas* rapidly acquired the renown and sanctity usually reserved for compositions in Sanskrit. Over the next three centuries its fame grew steadily, spread by oral expounders, itinerant singers, and scholarly exegetes. In the twentieth century it assumed an important place in the emerging Hindi literary canon, inspired major works by modernist poets, and was regularly quoted during India's freedom struggle by Mohandas Gandhi, who wrote that he considered it "the greatest book of all devotional literature."[2]

A retelling of the ancient and popular tale of Ram and Sita, which first appeared in literary form in Valmiki's Sanskrit epic *Rāmāyaṇa* (last centuries B.C.E.), the *Mānas* belongs to a long tradition of works that recast the narrative in distinctive ways. Tulsi's version comprises roughly 12,800 lines, divided into 1,073 "stanzas" set within seven sections. Apart from its basic storyline, the *Rāmcaritmānas* bears only an occasional direct resemblance to Valmiki's poem. Instead, drawing creatively on many sources, Tulsi retells the story of Ram through a set of four interlocking dialogues that ingeniously frame the epic tale: the conversations between the gods Shiva and Parvati, the Vedic sages Yajnavalkya and Bharadvaj, the immortal crow Bhushundi and the divine eagle Garuda, and finally the discourse of Tulsidas to his presumed audience.

Though warfare looms large in the sixth section in both the classical Sanskrit and Hindi epics, there are notable differences in how the two revered poets approached it. This portion of the story is the longest in Valmiki's masterpiece. In comparison, Tulsi's *Laṅkā-kāṇḍ* (the Lanka subbook) is short, and although it contains mas-

terful passages on the themes of statecraft and violence that are
said to dominate Valmiki's text, they are often greatly condensed
by Tulsi. Instead, the poet and his several narrators regularly pause,
even in the midst of battle, to meditate on Ram's beauty and gra-
ciousness—the latter is notably extended to Ram's demonic foes,
to whom he invariably grants an exalted spiritual state after slaying
them. Indeed Ram's divinity is always foregrounded.

When "The Siege of Lanka" opens, Ram and his armies of mon-
keys and bears have arrived at Lanka to wage war against the demon
Ravan, who has kidnapped Ram's wife Sita. On the second day of
battle, Ram's brother Lakshman is mortally wounded and Hanu-
man undertakes a voyage to retrieve the miraculous herb that can
save the stricken hero, provided it is administered to him before
dawn.

THE SIEGE OF LANKA

When he had received intelligence of the foe,
Ram summoned all his counselors and said,
"Lanka has four formidable gates;
consider how to lay siege to them."
Then the monkey and bear kings, with Vibhishan,
hearts focused on the jewel of the solar line,
pondered and arrived at the strategy
of forming their simian host into four divisions,
to which they appointed suitable generals.
Then they summoned all their commanders
and admonished them to recall the Lord's might.

The monkeys heard and rushed forth, roaring like lions.
Joyously, they bowed their heads at Ram's feet,
then, seizing mountaintops, the heroes surged forward.
Bellowing and reviling the foe, those bears and monkeys
shouted, "Victory to the Raghu hero, Kosala's king!"
Knowing Lanka to be an impregnable fortress,
they advanced fearlessly by the power of the Lord.
Like dense clouds, they hemmed the city on all sides,
emitting cries like resounding war drums.

"Victory to Ram, victory to Lakshman,
and victory to Sugriv, king of monkeys!"
Such were the lion-like roars of those simians
and bears, paragons of might.

A great commotion broke out in Lanka,
but when he heard it, Ten-head said arrogantly,
"Just look at the impudence of those apes,"
and laughing, summoned his night-stalker legions.
"These monkeys have come, driven by their doom,
and all my night-roaming demons are famished."
Then, roaring with laughter, the villain declared,
"Destiny delivers our meals while we sit at home.
Go forth, all you warriors, in the four directions,
seize those bears and monkeys, and devour them all."
Shiva said, "Uma, in his deluded arrogance, Ravan
was like the lapwing bird, which sleeps upside-down."[3]
At his command, the night-stalkers streamed forth
bearing slingshots and pointed javelins,

lances, maces, sharpened battle-axes,
spears, short swords, pikes, and boulders.[4]
As when, spying a field of reddish-colored rocks,
carnivorous birds foolishly fall upon them,
heedless of the pain of breaking their beaks,
just so did the crazed demons race forward.

Bearing all sorts of weapons and armed
with arrows and bows, mighty demon heroes,
steadfast in battle, in their tens of millions
climbed onto the ramparts of the fort.

The ramparts and parapets now appeared like
Mount Meru's summits wreathed in dark clouds.
Kettledrums and other martial instruments boomed,
exciting the hearts of heroes.
Countless drums and reeds were played
with a sound to rend the hearts of cowards.
Now the demons beheld that horde
of huge-bodied monkey and bear warriors
rushing forward, heedless of the rough terrain—
they just tore off mountaintops to make a path.
Gnashing their teeth, those millions of soldiers roared,[5]
bit their lips, and yelled in furious challenge.
There Ravan, and here Ram was loudly hailed,
and amid cries of "Victory! Victory!" battle was joined.
The demons sent down a barrage of craggy boulders,
but the monkeys leaped up, seized them, and threw them
  back.

Seizing chunks of mountain, the raging monkeys
and bears hurled them at the fortress.
Pouncing, they seized foes by the feet and slammed them
to the ground, and then ran off, roaring in challenge.
Extremely agile, young, and strong, and fired with rage,
those monkeys and bears climbed relentlessly
onto the citadel, and then onto houses, too,
everywhere proclaiming Ram's glorious renown.

Then each monkey, seizing a night-stalker,
leaped downward once more—
himself on top, his soldier-foe beneath—
and plunged to earth.

Empowered by Ram's might, the monkey legions
decimated hordes of demonic warriors
and, clambering onto the fort again from all sides,
shouted, "Victory to the Raghu hero, sun of splendor!"
The night-stalkers turned and fled pell-mell,
like cloudbanks driven by a powerful wind.
Great cries of lamentation arose in the city
as anguished women and children sobbed.[6]
With one voice, they all began cursing Ravan:
"Even while he reigns, he obstinately invites doom!"
When he got word of his army's disarray,
the enraged lord of Lanka sent his stalwarts back,
saying, "Anyone whom I hear of fleeing battle,
I will personally gut with my sharpest dagger.
You lapped up my largesse, enjoyed every comfort;
now, on the field, you cherish your own breath?"

When they heard these harsh words, all the soldiers,
frightened and ashamed, went back with renewed rage.
Thinking, "A hero's glory is to die in close combat,"
they relinquished all attachment to their lives.

Seizing diverse weapons and bellowing challenges,
those warriors all fell to fighting
the bears and monkeys, harassing them
with blows of their iron cudgels and tridents.

Seized with terror, the monkeys started to flee—
"Although, Uma," Shiva said, "they will eventually win."[7]
Some cried, "Where is Angad?" or "Where is Hanuman?"
"Where are the mighty Nal, Nil, and Dvivid?"
When Hanuman heard of the dismay of his troops,
that powerful one was at the western gate,
where he was doing battle with Meghnad,
but the gate did not fall, and there was great danger.
Then the son of the wind grew utterly enraged,
and roaring like all-powerful Death, that warrior
leaped atop the wall of Lanka's fortress,
seized a mountain peak, and charged at Meghnad.
He smashed his chariot, slew its driver,
and planted a mighty kick in the demon's chest.
A second driver, realizing the prince's distress,
put him in his chariot and rushed him home.

Angad heard that the son of the wind
had ventured alone onto the battlements.

Then Bali's son, too, adept in warfare,
mounted them with a playful simian leap.

Both monkeys, inflamed by battle passion,
yet inwardly meditating on Ram's majesty,
charged forward and climbed onto Ravan's palace,
proclaiming the victory of Kosala's king.
Seizing it by its spires, they toppled the building,
and to see this gave the night-stalker ruler a scare.
His women beat their breasts and wailed,
"Now two of those dreadful monkeys have come!"
Terrifying them with simian antics,
the two extolled the glory of Ramchandra.
Then they took hold of some gilded columns
and said, "Let's start wreaking real havoc."
Roaring, they plunged into enemy ranks
and began slaying them with their mighty arms.
Kicking some and slapping others, they said,
"Take your reward for not worshiping Ram!"

Smashing one demon against another,
they tore off their heads, then pitched them
so they landed right in front of Ravan,
where they burst like big clay pots of curd.

Finding demon generals, they seized them
by their feet and hurled them before the Lord.
Vibhishan identified them all by name,
and Ram admitted them to his own blessed abode.
Vile man-eaters, who feasted on twice-born flesh,

obtained that state for which yogis plead.
Shiva said, "Ram is tenderhearted and merciful, Uma,
and thought, 'In animosity, these demons remember me.'[8]
Reflecting thus, he gave them the supreme state—
tell me, Bhavani, who else is so compassionate?
Hearing this of the Lord, one who does not shed illusion
and worship him is an utterly luckless dolt."
"Angad and Hanuman have managed to enter
the citadel"—so the master of Avadh declared.
There in Lanka the two monkeys looked as splendid
as dual Mount Mandaras churning the milky sea.[9]

Having smashed enemy forces with the might
of their arms, and seeing that day was waning,
the two leaped down with untired ease
and came to where the blessed Lord was.

They bowed their heads at his holy feet,
and the Raghu lord rejoiced to see these champions.
As Ram gazed compassionately on the pair,
they became free of fatigue and blissfully happy.
Knowing that Angad and Hanuman had left,
countless bear and monkey soldiers turned back,
but the demons, gaining strength as day waned,[10]
charged again, proclaiming their ten-headed king's glory.
Seeing the night-stalker legions, the monkeys returned,
and warriors clashed everywhere, gnashing their teeth.
Both sides, equally powerful, roared in challenge,
and the dueling champions never admitted defeat.
The night-stalker heroes were all swarthy-limbed,

the simians, huge and multicolored.
Both armies were strong, with warriors of equal might,
and fought, in their rage, with reckless heroism,
as if dark monsoon clouds and multihued ones of Sharad[11]
were clashing, driven by powerful winds.
The demon generals Akampan and Atikay,[12]
their army faltering, resorted to magic.
In an instant, it became pitch-black
and began to rain blood, stone, and ash.

Seeing utter darkness in the ten directions,
the monkey army fell into a panic.
Unable to see one another,
they called frantically in every direction.

But the Raghu master knew the whole secret.
He summoned Angad and Hanuman
and explained it all to them.
When they heard, the mighty monkeys
        rushed off, enraged.
Then the merciful one laughed, raised his bow,
and quickly released a fiery arrow.
There was dazzling light, darkness was no more—
as when wisdom dawns, doubt departs.
Regaining light, the bears and monkeys
advanced happily, free of fatigue and fear.
Hanuman and Angad roared on the field,
and just hearing their battle cry, the demons fled.
Catching the fleeing troops, knocking them to the ground,
the bears and monkeys performed marvelous deeds:

seizing their feet, they hurled them into the sea,
where crocodiles, serpents, and sharks caught and ate
  them.[13]

Some were slaughtered, some badly wounded,
some ran away and clambered into the fort.
The bears and monkeys bellowed in triumph,
having scattered, by their might, the foe's army.
Knowing night had fallen, the four monkey legions
returned to where Kosala's king was camped,
and as soon as Ram's gracious glance fell on them
all those forest creatures shed their fatigue.
Back in Lanka, Ravan yelled for his advisers
and told them all of the champions who were slain.
"Those monkeys have massacred half our army!
Tell me, quickly, what strategy to execute."
Malyavant, a most venerable night-stalker,
Ravan's maternal grandfather and trusted minister,[14]
spoke up, giving most prudent counsel.
"Now just listen a bit, son, to my advice:
Ever since you stole Sita and brought her here,
there have been ill omens, too many to recount.
He whose fame Veda and *purāṇas* declare
is Ram, and no foe of his has ever won happiness.

He who slew the golden-eyed demon and his brother,
and mighty Madhu and Kaitabh, too—
that same supreme Lord, ocean of mercy,
has come down and taken birth once more.[15]

He who is Death himself, incinerating forests of sinners,
the abode of virtues, perfect enlightenment,
and who is worshiped by Shiva and Brahma—
how can he be opposed?

So give up your hostility, give back Vaidehi,*
and give praise to that most loving sea of mercy."
His words stung like arrows, and Ravan said,
"Blacken your face and go away, accursed one!
If you were not so aged, I would kill you—
now, don't ever show me your face again."
Hearing this from Ravan, Malyavant surmised
that the treasury of grace was bent on slaying him.
Scolding Ravan, he arose and departed.
Then prince Meghnad spoke up in anger:
"Just see what feats I will perform, come morning!
I will do far more than my words could say."
His son's speech brought Ravan confidence,
and he affectionately seated him on his lap.
They pondered and conferred till dawn broke
and the monkeys again assailed the four gates.
Enraged simians surrounded that formidable fortress,
and within the city there was terrible tumult.
Bearing all sorts of weapons, night-stalkers advanced
and rained down craggy boulders from the ramparts.
They hurled down millions of mountain peaks
and many kinds and sizes of iron balls

———

* Sita.

that crashed like lightning bolts and thundered
like the clouds that bring on world dissolution.
The furious monkey soldiers fought with ferocity,
despite bodies riddled with wounds, and never faltered.
Seizing summits, they hurled them at the fort,
slaying night-stalkers wherever they stood.

When Meghnad heard the report
that the fortress was again surrounded,
that hero descended from the citadel
and came forward, bellowing:

"Where are those two brothers, lords of Kosala,
renowned as bowmen in all the worlds?
Where are Nal, Nil, Dvivid, and Sugriva,
and those paragons of might, Angad and Hanuman?
And where is Vibhishan, that disloyal brother?
Today I vow to kill you all, and especially him!"
So saying he readied his cruel arrows,
and in fury, drew his bow-string to its full extent.[16]
He released a great volley of arrows
that raced off like countless winged serpents.
Everywhere, monkeys were seen being felled
and none, at that moment, could dare face him.
Monkeys and bears began fleeing in all directions,
forgetting their determination to give battle.
On the whole field, no monkey or bear could be seen
whom he had not left just barely alive.

He struck each one of them with ten arrows
and the monkey heroes tumbled to the ground.
Then Meghnad, mighty and resolute,
roared in triumph like a lion.

Seeing the army in distress, the son of the wind
was enraged and charged like Death himself.
He quickly uprooted a huge mountain
and in a fury hurled it at Meghnad,
who, seeing it coming, rose into the sky,
sacrificing his chariot, driver, and horses.
Though Hanuman challenged him time and again,
he would not come near, knowing the monkey's might.
Then Meghnad approached the Raghu lord,
taunting him with innumerable insults
and showering him with all kinds of weapons.
But the Lord, in mere play, broke and deflected them.
The fool, abashed at seeing such power,
began deploying many kinds of illusions,
like one who, taking on great Garuda,
brandishes a baby snake to frighten him.[17]

Before him—whose maya holds sway over all,
great and small, not excepting Shiva and Brahma—
that deluded night-stalker displayed
his own paltry magic.

Soaring into the sky, he rained down burning coals,
as great jets of water burst out of the earth
and countless kinds of male and female goblins[18]

danced about shrieking, "Kill! Maim!"
Feces, pus, blood, hair, and bones pelted down,
interspersed with torrents of rock and ash.
Then he released dust so thick that darkness fell
and none could see even his own outstretched hand.
When they saw these illusions, the monkeys grew
    distraught
and reckoned they all were surely doomed.
Beholding this farce, Ram merely smiled,
yet he knew that all his monkeys were terrified.
With a single arrow, he cut through the demonic maya
as the day-bringing sun dispels dense darkness.
Then he cast so gracious a look over monkeys and bears
that, reenergized, they could not be stopped on the field.

Asking Ram's permission, and accompanied
by Angad and other monkeys,
Lakshman went forth in anger,
taking up his arrows and bow.

His eyes were red, his chest broad, arms thick,
and his body, fair as Himalaya's snow, was slightly flushed.
For his part, Ravan dispatched stalwart warriors
who raced forth clutching countless armaments.
With weapons of crags, tree trunks, and their own nails,
the monkeys charged, shouting, "Victory to Ram!"
Clashing, they all squared off in single combats,
with both sides equally intent on triumphing.
Pounding with fists and feet, biting with their teeth,

the monkeys, sure of victory, pummeled and taunted
    them.
"Strike!" "Kill!" "Seize and destroy!"
"Tear off his head!" "Grab his arms and rip them out!"
—such cries permeated all the nine regions,[19]
as headless torsos raced wildly here and there.
Watching the spectacle from the sky, the host of gods
was at times anxious, at times delighted.

Blood collected to fill all pits in the field,
and over them, dust blew,
so they looked like beds of glowing embers
shrouded in cremation smoke.[20]

With their streaming wounds, heroes appeared
like flame-of-the-forest trees in full bloom.[21]
The two warriors Lakshman and Meghnad
struggled with each other in immense rage,
yet neither one could triumph.
The night-stalker fought wickedly, using deceit,
but then endless Anant* grew enraged[22]
and quickly destroyed his chariot and driver.
Shesh assaulted him in countless ways,
so that the demon barely clung to his breath.
That son of Ravan thought to himself,
"This is serious—he looks to take my life!"
Then he hurled the spear called "hero-slayer"—
a mass of fiery energy that lodged in Lakshman's chest.

* Lakshman.

He fainted when that weapon struck,
and his foe grew bold and approached him.

A billion demon warriors equal to Meghnad
tried to pick him up,
but how could they lift Shesh, support of the world?[23]
Abashed, they all slunk away.

Shiva said, "Girija, he whose anger is the fire
that instantly incinerates the fourteen worlds—
who could truly defeat in battle the one
who is worshiped by gods, mortals, and all beings?[24]
This marvel can be comprehended only
by one who has received Ram's grace."
As twilight fell, the two armies retreated
and began accounting for their legions.
The all-pervading God, unassailable Lord of the worlds,
and treasury of mercy asked, "Where is Lakshman?"
Then Hanuman brought him in, and at the sight[25]
of his young brother, the Lord felt intense sorrow.
Jambavan said, "The physician Sushen[26]
resides in Lanka. Who can be sent to fetch him?"
Assuming tiny form, Hanuman went
and brought him at once, house and all.

Sushen approached and bowed
his head at Ram's blessed feet.
Then he named a mountain and healing herb
and said, "Go, son of the wind, and bring it."[27]

Focusing his heart on Ram's holy feet
and affirming his own might, the tempest's son left.[28]
But back in Lanka, a spy reported the matter,
and then Ravan came to Kalnemi's abode.
Ten-head told him everything, and, listening,
Kalnemi beat his brow in despair and said,
"He who burned the city right before your eyes—
who is going to be able to obstruct his path?
For your own good, worship the Raghu lord
and give up your vain boasting, master.
His dark body, lovely as a blue lotus,
enchants the eyes—set it in your heart.
Renounce the folly of dualism and greed,[29]
and awake from your sleep in delusion's night.
He who devours the serpent of deadly time—
can anyone even dream of defeating him in battle?"

Listening to him, the ten-necked one grew enraged,
and Kalnemi thought to himself,
"Better to die at the hand of Ram's messenger;
this villain is mired in a mass of sin."

With this, he went and fabricated an illusion
on Hanuman's way—a lake, shrine, and lovely garden.
The son of the wind saw the hermitage and thought,
"I will ask the sage for water to dispel my fatigue."
The demon, in false guise, looked splendid there—
trying to trick the messenger of maya's own Lord.
When the son of the wind presented his respects,
that "sage" began singing of Ram's virtues, saying,

"There is now a great battle between Ravan and Ram,
in which Ram will triumph—no doubt about that.
Though I stay here, I can see it all, brother,
for I possess immense powers of inner vision."
Hanuman asked for water and the sage offered his pot,[30]
but the monkey said, "So little water won't sate my thirst."
"Then go bathe in the lake," the other said, "and return at
     once;
I will initiate you so you acquire knowledge."[31]

As soon as the monkey stepped into the lake,
a frenzied female crocodile seized his foot.
When he killed her, she assumed a divine form
and rose skyward on a celestial chariot,

saying, "Seeing you, monkey, I am freed of sin,
and a great sage's curse is removed, brother.[32]
But this one is no sage; he's a cruel night-stalker.
Know my words to be true, monkey."
No sooner had the *apsarā*, saying this, left,
than the monkey went to that night-stalker
and said, "Take my guru gift now, sage,[33]
and you can give me your mantra later."
Wrapping his tail around his head, Hanuman felled him,
and as he died, the demon showed his true form.
Crying, "Ram, Ram!" he gave up his life—
Hanuman heard this and left, well content.[34]
He saw the peak, but could not recognize the herb,
so he impulsively tore out the whole mountain,

and grasping it, was racing back through the night sky
when the monkey passed over Avadh city.

Bharat saw that enormous shape
and, guessing it might be a night-stalking demon,
took up a blunt arrow,
drew his bow-string to its full extent, and fired.

At the arrow's impact, Hanuman fell to earth senseless,
yet repeating, "Ram, Ram, lord of the Raghus."
Hearing those dear words, Bharat leaped up
and anxiously hurried to where the monkey lay,
saw his distress, and hugged him to his breast,
but despite all efforts, he could not be aroused.
With stricken face and a heavy heart,
Bharat spoke, his eyes filling with tears:
"The cruel destiny that turned me against Ram
now gives me this further, awful sorrow.
But if, in my mind, speech, and bodily acts
I have only guileless love for Ram's holy feet,
may this monkey be free of distress and pain—
yes, if the Raghu lord is pleased with me."
As soon as he heard this, that lord of monkeys sat up
crying, "Victory! Victory to the king of Kosala!"

Then Bharat again held the monkey to his heart,
his body thrilling, eyes flooded with tears,
and heart unable to contain the love he felt
in recalling Ram, crown jewel of the Raghu line.[35]

"Tell me, friend," he asked, "how he is—the abode
of bliss—with our young brother and Mother Janaki."
As Hanuman narrated all their deeds in brief,
Bharat grew depressed and repentant at heart,
and thought, "Alas, Fate! Why was I born in this world,
unable to be of even the least service to the Lord?"
Yet understanding the crisis, he took courage,
and then that mighty hero addressed Hanuman:
"Friend, your arrival will be delayed
and your mission will fail if dawn breaks.
So climb, with your mountain, onto my arrow,
and I will propel you there, to the abode of mercy."
Hearing this, a conceit arose in the monkey's heart:
"How, with my weight, will an arrow move?"
But then, reflecting on Ram's infinite power,
he bowed at Bharat's feet, and humbly said,

"My lord, keeping your might in my heart,[36]
I will proceed there at once, master."
So saying, and taking Bharat's leave,
Hanuman bowed at his feet and departed.

The strength of Bharat's arms, his nobility, virtue,
and limitless love for the Lord's feet—
inwardly praising all these again and again,
the son of the wind sped on.

Meanwhile Ram, gazing at Lakshman,
grieved like an ordinary man, saying,

"Half the night is gone and the monkey is not back."
Ram lifted his young brother to his breast.
"You could never bear to see me suffer,
brother, and your disposition was always mild.
For my sake, you left your father and mother
to endure cold, heat, and harsh wind in the forest.
But where is that ardor now, dear brother?
Why don't you rise, hearing my anguished words?
Had I known that I would lose my brother in exile,
I would not have heeded those orders from father.[37]
Sons, wealth, wife, home, and family
come and go, time and again in this world.
Awaken, dear one, reflecting on this:
a blood brother is not easily found on earth![38]
Wretched as a wingless bird, a king cobra
without its gem, or a trunkless great elephant,
so will my life be without you, brother,
should senseless fate somehow keep me alive.
How can I show my face, going back to Avadh,
having lost, for a woman's sake, a dear brother?
Better that I endure disgrace in the world
for forfeiting a wife, which is no great loss.
Now, dishonor, as well as grief for you, child,
this cruel, hard heart of mine will have to bear.
You are your mother's only son,[39]
dear one, and the support of her very life.
She took your hand and entrusted you to me,
believing I would ensure your welfare and happiness.
Going back to her, how will I answer for myself?
Brother, why do you not rise and instruct me?"

Thus the liberator from grief grieved in many ways,
as his eyes, large and lovely as lotus petals, shed tears.
But, Uma, the Raghu king is the one, indivisible reality,
who displays human ways out of mercy for devotees.

Listening to the Lord's lamentations,
the army of monkeys grew anguished.
Just then, Hanuman arrived,
like the heroic mood bursting into a scene of pathos.[40]

Ram embraced Hanuman with delight,
for the all-knowing Lord was profoundly grateful.
Then the physician quickly applied the remedy
and Lakshman sat up, free of distress.
The Lord hugged his brother to his heart
as the legions of bears and monkeys rejoiced.
Then Hanuman returned the physician to Lanka
exactly as he had previously brought him.
When the ten-headed king heard this news,
he despaired and repeatedly beat his brow.
Then, greatly upset, he went to Kumbhakaran,
and using all sorts of efforts, woke him up.

8.

Selections from
The History of Akbar

by Abu'l-Fazl

*Translated from Persian
by Wheeler M. Thackston*

Abu'l-Fazl (1551–1602) was born in the capital city of the Mughal
empire, Agra. He was introduced to the court in 1574 by his elder
brother, the poet laureate Abu'l-Faiz "Faizi." In 1588 Abu'l-Fazl
was commanded by the Mughal emperor Akbar to write a history
of the reigns of the Timurid sovereigns of India, and the following
year another edict was issued to the same purpose. The result was
The History of Akbar (*Akbarnāma*). He was killed in 1602 in retali-
ation for his opposition to the succession of Prince Salim, the fu-
ture Emperor Jahangir, who was in open rebellion against his father
at the time. The prince contrived to have a Bundela chieftain, Bir
Singh Deo, assassinate Abu'l-Fazl as he was returning to the capital
from the Deccan.[1]

The History of Akbar begins with Akbar's birth and his horo-
scopes and traces Akbar's ancestors, from Adam to his grandfather
Babur and father Humayun. It then records his accession to the
throne in 1556 and continues chronologically through each regnal

year. After Abu'l-Fazl's murder, another writer extended the work to cover the remainder of Akbar's lifetime through 1605.

Abu'l-Fazl's work is far from a simple recording of history. It represents an attempt on his part to apotheosize Akbar. Not merely the third monarch of the Mughal Empire in India, Akbar became, in Abu'l-Fazl's hands, the latest and most perfect manifestation of the divine light that had infused Alanqoa, the remote ancestress of both Genghis Khan and Tamerlane, and that continued, hidden, in the lineage for many generations until it attained perfection and was revealed in the person of Akbar.[2]

Abu'l-Fazl portrays Akbar as the ideal monarch, drawing from the models of both ancient Iranian kingship and the perfect man in Sufism. He associates Akbar's birth with supernatural occurrences and miracles, as is usually done in recounting the birth of a prophet or deity.

Akbar's achievements as the Muslim ruler of a polity of non-Muslim-majority people were prodigious and left a legacy that endured into the colonial and postindependence periods. He incorporated the northern part of the subcontinent, from Kabul to Bengal, into the Mughal Empire, and effected changes in the assessment and collection of taxes, the organization and control of the nobility, and the reform of the state's religious policies. He made marriage alliances with Rajput clans, thus paving the way for the integration of Timurid culture in India.

Akbar was supported by Abu'l-Fazl in challenging the influential court clergy and fighting bigotry among all religious communities. There were two notable episodes in the furthering of Akbar's policy of universal concord (*sulh-i kull*) that had both political and religious considerations behind them. One was the establishment of the house of worship (*'ibādatkhāna*) for weekly discussions among Sufis, Hindus, Jains, Jesuits, and Zoroastrians, out of which Akbar's short-lived syncretistic religious doctrine of the "divine religion" (*dīn-i ilāhī*) emerged. The other was the "translation bureau" (*maktabkhāna*), which chiefly sponsored translations of works of Hindu learning into Persian. In terms of cultural artifacts and material wealth, the Mughals at this time far outshone the Ottoman and Safavid empires. Many scholars and poets from Iran and Central Asia settled in India, drawn by the lavish patronage offered by Akbar and other Mughal nobles, and contributed to the cosmopolitan nature of the literary culture. It was in this environment that *The History of Akbar* was written. Several copies of the work were illustrated by renowned artists in the royal atelier.

The writing style adopted by Abu'l-Fazl is no less grandiose than his aim. There are digressions and soliloquies. Except when he is dealing with straightforward historical narrative, Abu'l-Fazl writes in a parabolic style that is far from immediately comprehensible; not only is the style difficult but he also coins new words and uses old ones in novel ways. In his writing Abu'l-Fazl borrowed from the vocabulary of Sufism, which had suffused Persian poetry and become part and parcel of the lexicon of a normal Persian literary education, and adapted it to his purposes. Primarily this refers to Akbar's own quest, but to know that Akbar is a manifestation of divine wisdom is, for Abu'l-Fazl, the supreme realization.[3]

Disinterested, unbiased reporting is not for Abu'l-Fazl. For him, any expansion of territory that brings the order bestowed by the "wisdom-adorning one who graces the throne" to the benighted world of chaos outside the cradle of empire is not merely praiseworthy but a true "act of divine worship" (*'ibādat*).

INSURRECTION IN MALWA

In good conscience a ruler cosnsiders it obligatory to be constantly informed of his realm and the nobles of his state, particularly of the headstrong of limited competence who enjoy fortune but have drifted away from the immediate vicinity of the throne, so that they can be dealt with before they cause trouble. Thank God this great characteristic exists in His Imperial Majesty to such perfection that even the wisest are incapable of comprehending it. He constantly seeks information on the hidden things of the kingdom, and while outwardly he engages in hunts and such activities, he merely uses them as pretexts and does not neglect the important affairs of religion and state for even an instant, for he always has his attention focused on the worship of God and taking care of his subjects. Therefore, when at this point it reached the imperial hearing that Abdullah Khan Uzbek, who had partaken of the imperial table of fortune, had reared his head in insurrection in Malwa and was so incompetent that he was about to throw off the mantle of imperial favor in ingratitude, the emperor set out for an elephant hunt on an expedition to Malwa.

With divine assistance, on Bahram day, the twentieth of Tir, corresponding to Saturday the twenty-first of Dhu'l-Qa'da [July 1, 1564], during the season when the reeling elephants of clouds cast intoxicated roars to the earth, drip drunkenly from time to time, and cause such torrents to flow that uphill cannot be distinguished from downhill, and so refractory are they that they do not obey the goads of lightning, the imperial banners set off for Narwar and Sipri, where there are forests with elephants. When the imperial train was camped beside the Chambal River, it rained so hard that the river overflowed its banks. It took nearly two weeks to get the camp across by boat. While the royal elephants were crossing the churning river, a renowned elephant named Lakhna drowned. From there the train proceeded to Gwalior, where it camped. From there the pleasant expanses in the vicinity of the Narwar fortress became the site of the imperial tents.

With elephant forests nearby, the emperor set out to hunt and divided the members of the retinue into several platoons, each led by one of the amirs, and with them he sent several tame and obedient elephants. They were also provided with strong, thick ropes capable of holding these enormous beasts. The emperor ordered that when a wild elephant was found, a tame elephant should be driven after it long enough for the wild beast to be driven to exhaustion. Then elephant keepers riding tame elephants should close in on both sides of the wild one, throw ropes around its neck, and tie the ropes securely to the tame elephants' necks. Having captured a wild elephant in this manner, they were to drive their elephants and pull the wild one in. Gradually, day by day, they would approach nearer the wild elephant with gentleness and put fodder before it so that little by little they would be able to mount it and tame it in a short span of time. The basic technique of taming any wild animal is through gentleness and by giving it straw, grain, and water appropriate to its nature. By analogy, this is also the easiest method of hunting elephants, for a wild elephant is a huge, powerful beast that can only be made obedient and tamed by an elephant more powerful than or equal to it. By this means they achieve their goals.

Intent upon hunting elephants in the forests of Narwar, the emperor dispatched platoons in every direction while he himself and his elite entered the forest. After much searching a female elephant appeared in the distance. Rushing after it and tiring it out, they tied it to another elephant. While it was being tied, Mulla Kitabdar's son Adham fell under the elephant's feet and was stepped on, but he scrambled to safety. The next day was the Feast of the Sacrifice. Mun'im Khan Khankhanan, who was attending the emperor during the hunt, came with the members of the retinue to kiss the ground and offer congratulations. The emperor set out again to hunt elephants. Every platoon went off in the direction it had been assigned. That day, after much effort, a herd of female elephants with two or three males was located. Delighted by the sight, the emperor captured all nine. The next day he remained in the royal tents to tend to administrative affairs, a type of spiritual hunt. On the third morning he mounted with the first light of dawn and rode until the end of the day through the jungle, which was so thick with trees and laced with branches that it would be difficult for a breeze to get through. Suddenly he came across a herd of more than seventy elephants. Exhibiting great joy, he took it as a good omen of lofty goals. By His Imperial Majesty's order all the elephants were driven into the thick jungle, the legs of each elephant were tied to a tree, and guards were set to keep watch while ropes were brought from the camp. That night the jungle, in which human had never set foot and which fleet imagination had never traversed, became a metropolis with the arrival of the imperial train. Expert carpet spreaders and carpenters constructed a lofty dais of wood covered with fine fabric for the emperor's rest. His intimates, like Yusuf-Muhammad Khan Kökältash, Aziz-Muhammad Kökältash, Yusuf Khan Kökältash, Mir Mu'iz-zulmulk, Mir Ali-Akbar, Chalma Khan (who had been entitled Khan Alam), Mir Ghiyasuddin Ali (who has now been entitled

Naqib Khan), and others, encircled the emperor.

When the sun rose the next day the emperor sat on the throne, kindly ordered those present to sit, and enjoyed listening to Darbar Khan as he related stories of Amir Hamza for a while. Meanwhile several elephants arrived from the camp with many ropes. An order was given for each of the refractory and mighty wild elephants to be tied tightly between two royal elephants and driven till evening to the vicinity of the imperial camp. Ropes like rogues' lassoes were thrown around those mountainous beasts and secured, and the camp remained there for the two days it took to accomplish this task.

Since the emperor desired to hunt some more wild beasts, he set out toward Malwa. On account of the lightning and heavy rain, torrents, mud, and mire, and because of the pits and cavities with which the terrain of Malwa is filled, it was laborious to proceed. Their mounts swam like sea horses, and the camels crossed the floods like ocean-going ships until, with great difficulty, camp was pitched on the outskirts of the town of Ranod. They remained there for two days on account of the rain. Proceeding from there toward Sarangpur, they encountered so much mud and mire on the road that the fleet-footed stallions sank to their chests in the mud and the camels were so weighed down by their own coats that they could scarcely move. On this day the imperial tents lagged behind. Other than the emperor's own tent and canopy, a tent for the khankhanan, one for Mirza Aziz Kökältash, and those of several other amirs, no one's tent arrived. Consequently a halt of one day was observed there.

The next day they proceeded toward Mandu, and in five stations the outskirts of the town of Khairar became the site of the imperial camp. Although the animals had found no grain so far, the fresh green fields growing in this area recompensed them well and made them forget their desire for grain. They all put their heads down in the fields and ate their fill of delicious grass.

His Imperial Majesty turned his attention from hunting, left the camp there under the charge of several amirs, and galloped toward Mandu, the seat of the headstrong Abdullah Khan. Along the way he sent Ashraf Khan and I'timad Khan forward to warn Abdullah Khan of his inappropriate actions, to bring him to pay homage in hopes of imperial favor, and not to allow him to become lost in the wilderness of misfortune. The emperor set out through all that water and mud on wings of haste for one station from Khairar to Sarangpur, the first city in Malwa, twenty-five leagues from Malwa itself and forty leagues from Delhi. In the Sarangpur vicinity Muhammad Qasim Khan Nishapuri, who held the governorship of that area, came out to greet the emperor and beg him to stop at his quarters. Before the emperor's gaze he paraded nearly seven hundred horses and pack animals belonging to himself and his retainers. The emperor gradually awarded them to the members of the retinue during this expedition. At dawn the emperor mounted and set off for Ujjain, the former capital of the rulers of Malwa. When the air of Dhar was perfumed by the imperial advent, Ashraf Khan and I'timad Khan came from Abdullah Khan to report what had happened. No matter how much these loyal diplomats had talked, it had made no impression on his hypocritical make-up. He had sent his belongings out of the fortress, waited until nightfall, and then gone out after his men. He had made some silly requests to get the emissaries out of his hair. For instance, he had asked that no financial or mortal injury should come to him, the province of Mandu should be his as before, and Tängriberdi, Khanqulï, and

Esän Bakhshi should be left with him. Trusting in the emperor's innate clemency, Munʿim Khan Khankhanan requested that Abdullah Khan's offenses be forgiven. His Imperial Majesty kindly pardoned him and granted his requests, and an edict to that effect was sent with Iʿtimad Khan and Darbar Khan.

While the emperor was camped in Dhar, a tyrannized woman came with the following complaint: "Abdullah Khan's arms bearer, Muhammad Husain, has perpetrated all sorts of harassment upon my adolescent daughter and plundered my home."

His Imperial Majesty responded, saying, "Fret not. Expect the rising of the lights of justice, for soon we will subject him to great punishment." It is a testament to His Imperial Majesty's extraordinary foresight that the first person to be captured and sent to execution in retribution was he.

During this month it was reported to the emperor that when Abdullah Khan learned of the arrival of the imperial train, knowing that it meant his certain doom and seeing himself bound in chains by imperial wrath, he fled in fear and trepidation from Mandu to Lawani. From Mandu the emperor turned his reins to pursue the miscreant. A group of loyal amirs like Mir Muʿizzulmulk, Muqim Khan, Muhammad-Qasim Khan Nishapuri, Shah Fakhruddin, Shahqulï Khan Mahram, Dastam Khan, Maʿsum Khan Farankhudi, Qutlugh-Qadam Khan, Khurram Khan, Qilich Khan, Iʿtimad Khan, Chaghatai Khan, and some others were dispatched forward as a vanguard to ride fast and cut him off while the emperor and some of his intimates quickened their pace. At the end of Din day, the twenty-fourth of Amurdad, corresponding to Saturday the twenty-sixth of Dhu'l-Hijja [August 5, 1564], as night was falling, the emperor stopped at Liwani. The wretch had already fled. After remaining there that night, I'timad Khan and Darbar Khan, who had already tried to lead him onto the right way, were given leave to go get the miscreant on the right track with their good advice. The next morning the emperor proceeded from Liwani. Along the way the emissaries returned to report that Abdullah Khan's luck was so black that he had taken their advice to be treachery and turned his back on fortune. By chance, good luck led those who formed the vanguard to a village called Bagh, where it was learned that the miscreant had sent his baggage forward and stopped there. Coincidentally, due to the rough terrain, the men of the vanguard had swerved slightly from the direct way, and a few—like Muhammad-Qasim Khan Nishapur, Khan Alam, Shahqulï Khan Mahram, Samanchi Khan, Khwaja Abdullah, Mirzada Ali Khan, and Sayyid Abdullah had gone forward, provoked a battle, and trapped their quarry. The unfortunate Abdullah Khan, unaware of the divine hosts, had turned back to fight them, saying to his companions, "At such a juncture the imperial train has galloped a long way and come with few men. We are many and strong. Concentrate your efforts and go into battle!" With this incorrect thought in mind, he went spitefully into battle with his troops. When it was reported to the emperor by fleet-footed messengers that those who were supported by fortune had gone heroically and self-sacrificingly into battle, the banners of fortune also set out in haste. On this day Khaksar Sultan, in his incompetence and flawed knowledge, suggested that the emperor cease his gallop. Imperial wrath flared up, and he put his hand on his sword and turned to him in total ire. The fool got off his horse and disappeared amidst the soldiers' horses. The emperor also dismounted, caught up with him, and struck him with his sword. Since the blade was an Indian *khanda,* it did not kill him. When imperial clemency saw him fallen in the dust of humility, it protected him, and the emperor left him alone. Of course, this outburst of imperial wrath tempered by kindness was apropos so that everyone would know his own rank and speak accordingly, seeing that the emperor's own view is so farsighted. Not everyone who is worthy of liege service is appropriate for service in the imperial presence; not everyone who is worthy of joining the emperor's retinue is suitable for the carpet of honor; not everyone who is worthy of the carpet of fortune deserves to sit; not everyone who has the distinction of sitting in the emperor's presence has permission to speak, certainly not to the lord of the world; not everyone who has been given permission to speak is worthy of opposing imperial demands. As a rule, the audacity to oppose the exalted goals of emperors and to go against the opinions of the great is contrary to wisdom except when the great grant this level with their own comprehension to one of the farsighted of the carpet of honor and exalt him among their attendants. Then, if he speaks the truth in the garb of humility, he will have performed a good service.

THE BATTLE OF BAGH

In short, His Imperial Majesty had the imperial banners, which were inscribed with victory and triumph, move out and cast their shadows over the loyal warriors. The emperor himself entered the arena of victory and reached a place where one of the foe's arrows passed by his head, but divine protection shielded him from the shafts of adversity. To the emperor's right was Mun'im Khan Khankhanan, and on his other side was I'timad Khan. The battle was raging. By divine inspiration the emperor ordered the drums of victory to be sounded loudly, and His Imperial Majesty addressed the khankhanan, saying, "This is no place to stand still. One must attack the enemy." So saying, he began to loosen his reins. The khankhanan said meekly, "The imperial mind has had a good idea, but this is no time for riding alone. Let the self-sacrificing attendants group, and then we will attack."

At this point His Imperial Majesty angrily got ready to charge. I'timad Khan devotedly took hold of the emperor's reins, but the emperor repulsed him and started forward. Now the foe, seeing with their own eyes the imperial splendor and the emperor's battle-breaking attack, which not even a mountain could withstand, lost heart. The magnificent divine aura that accompanied the riders in the arena of high-mindedness picked up those ill-starred misfortunes and overturned them. Several of Abdullah Khan's important leaders were killed, and many were taken captive. A victory that could serve as a manual for all time appeared with the merest movement of fortune. On this day a glorious triumph was achieved by the loyal attendants at the threshold of fortune, who numbered no more than three hundred. Among them were the following:

Mun'im Khan Khankhanan
Mirza Aziz Kökältash
Saif Khan Kökältash
Muqim Khan
Muhammad-Qasim Khan Nishapuri

Mir Mu'izzulmulk
Mir Ali-Akbar
Shah Fakhruddin
Ashraf Khan
I'timad Khan
Khan Alam
Asaf Khan
Lashkar Khan
Shahqulï Khan Mahram
Dastam Khan
Ma'sum Khan Farankhudi
Qilich Khan
Rahmanqulï Khan Qushbegi
Khurram Khan
Qutlugh-Qadam Khan
Khwaja Abdullah
Hajji-Muhammad Khan Sistani
Adil, son of Shah-Muhammad Qandahari
Muttalib Khan
Chaghatai Khan
Raja Todar Mal
Rai Pitar Das
Khaksar
Wazir Jamil
Murad Beg

Despite the fact that the imperial army was extremely few in number, had traversed such a distance during such a season, and entered battle, and although the army of the foe faced them in total preparedness and numbered more than a thousand horsemen, victory was achieved through the power of divine assistance. When good fortune does its job, numerical superiority has no importance. When the masters of creation assist, how can earthlings hope to oppose?

To return to the story: after the defeat of the ill-starred wretch and the hoisting of the banner of victory, His Imperial Majesty spent the night there, dispatching several of his self-sacrificing commanders under the leadership of Qasim Khan Nishapuri to go in pursuit of the wretch. Since it rained heavily that night, some of those assigned to this task were unable to go more than four or five leagues. When it was light, the emperor decamped and sent messengers to the vanguard to be bold and advance to battle. Going in haste, the warriors set out in obedience, and on the morning of Ashtad day, the twenty-sixth of Amurdad, corresponding to Monday the twenty-eighth of Dhu'l-Hijja [August 7, 1564], the imperial banners reached Ali at the beginning of the third watch. Hakim Ainulmulk, who was acquainted with the raja of Ali, went to bring him to pay homage and join the posse. On this day, which was a time in which manliness and mettle were assessed, Temür Yaka proved cowardly: when the world lord gave him a royal horse and assigned him to go forward to reconnoiter, the reprobate's courage failed him, and he feigned illness. One watch of the night remained when the world lord mounted. Since the weather was hot, he stopped for a moment beneath a tree and assigned Khoshkhabar Khan to go quickly and bring news of the posse. The emperor was still there when Khoshkhabar Khan brought back the good news of victory.

In summary, the zamindars of the area joined the victorious troops in loyal service, and the warriors of the all-conquering army let out a battle cry and poured down on Abdullah Khan's camp near a hill from which Champaner could be seen. The ill-starred wretch lost his nerve, left his womenfolk in the wilderness, took his son along, and absconded. The great amirs gathered all his belongings and baggage, particularly his womenfolk and elephants, and stopped there. Mir Muʿizzulmulk and a group of amirs detached themselves and went in pursuit of the wretches for five leagues. Traveling on wings of fortune, they caught up with him and drove most of his men away. Mir Muʿizzulmulk and several others, to their credit, suffered wounds. The wretch got himself out of the fray more dead than alive, and since there was still a little life left in him, he managed to get to the border of Gujarat. Since the emperor had not ordered them to proceed, they stopped there. When the good news was relayed to the emperor he set out accompanied by good fortune and victory to that area and gave thanks. His loyal amirs kissed the emperor's carpet and presented for his inspection all the booty they had taken, women, elephants, horses, cash, goods, and valuables. Among them were the elephants Aprup, Gaj Gajhin, and Suman, each one of which attracted the emperor's attention, and truly they were marvels of creation.

After thanking God for his gifts, His Imperial Majesty had the drums sounded for the return to Mandu. The distance was covered in three stages, and on Marasfand day, the twenty-ninth of Amurdad, corresponding to Thursday the second of Muharram 972 [August 10, 1564], the Mandu fortress was graced by the emperor's advent. From there proclamations of victory were dispatched to all parts of the Protected Realm, especially to Agra, where Khwaja Jahan and Muzaffar Khan were taking care of the administration. The emperor enjoyed himself there for nearly a month while he inspiredly put the region in order and rewarded the members of the court according to their performance and level of service. Muqim Khan, who had performed outstandingly during this expedition, was awarded the title of Shaja'at Khan. Once the news of the emperor's presence had spread throughout the province of Malwa, the leaders and chieftains of the area came to prostrate themselves humbly, and the *rais* and zamindars exalted themselves by kissing the ground before the emperor.

While there, it was reported to court that Abdullah Khan had gone in defeat to Changiz Khan, who had reared his head in greatness in Gujarat. The emperor decided to send one of his competent diplomats to tell Changiz Khan either to send the miscreant to court in chains or exile him from his territory. Hakim Ainulmulk was dispatched with an imperial decree. Changiz Khan came out nearly as far as Champaner to greet the decree and displayed much flattery, and he sent some of his important men to court with appropriate tribute and a letter in which he protested his wretchedness. "I am the emperor's slave," the letter said. "I have no alternative but to obey. Inasmuch as the emperor is clement and generous, if this time His Majesty will pardon his crime and show favor so that I may send him to court, it would be a sign of kindness to a slave. If this request does not meet with acceptance, I must send the wretch out of this province." One day after the imperial banners turned back on the return journey from this expedition and reached Agra, Hakim Ainulmulk arrived with Changiz Khan's tribute.

9.

Selections from
Sufi Lyrics

by Bullhe Shah

*Translated from Panjabi
by Christopher Shackle*

———

Bullhe Shah (d. 1758) has long been rightly regarded as the greatest master of the mystical Sufi lyric in Panjabi, but remarkably few details of his life can be reliably established. The lyrics of Bullhe Shah and the other Sufi poets, who lived at different times and in different areas of Panjab, were never systematically preserved by an organized faith community, and they were for the most part recorded and assembled in printed collections only in the late nineteenth century.

Neither the exact date nor the precise place of his birth is known for certain. The title "Bullhe Shah," by which the poet is commonly known, is the honorific form proper to a Sayyid descendant of the prophet Muhammad. His usual poetic signature, "Bullha," is the familiar form of his given name, Abdullah. His poetry's main focus is on his spiritual guide, noted Sufi master Shah Inayat (d. 1728). Bullhe's repeated references to Shah Inayat testify to the passionate quality of his devotion to his master.[1]

Bullhe Shah's eighteenth-century poems have a direct and simple style that underpins their very strong appeal across religious and national boundaries. His Sufi lyrics, whether through performances by well-known Sikh or Muslim singers or through the popular selections issued by Indian and Pakistani publishers, continue to evoke a magical vision from the past of a timeless unity, transcending the fractures of modern conflicts in the Panjab region and resonating in the modern imagination. They are among the classics truly loved today, valued for their universal messages.

The primary genre for Sufi poetry was the ghazal, a short love lyric with a strongly marked single rhyme whose characteristic blending of divine and human love was endlessly explored in the prolific output of such different poets as Rumi and Amir Khusrau.[2]

The formal genres of Panjabi Sufi poetry fall into the same broad categories as much premodern bhakti verse and the compositions of the Sikh Gurus. The main lyrical form is a strophic poem with strongly rhymed verses and a refrain, called *kāfī*, which is designed for singing. Bullhe Shah is known primarily for his *kāfīs*.

Sufism in India is no exception to the general rule that Sufism is and always has been an integral part of Islam. Although so different from orthodox scholars, the Sufis, in their emphasis on the primacy of spiritual understanding, like the scholars, found their core inspiration in the message of the Qur'an and the example of the prophet Muhammad.[3] Italics are used here to mark Bullhe Shah's citation of Qur'anic verses and other Arabic sayings.[4] His poetic references also extend beyond the Islamic tradition to include occasional references to figures from the Hindu world.[5]

Absolute authenticity in the precise wording of any poem generally agreed to be by Bullhe Shah is hardly to be expected, given the liberties taken by professional singers and the uncertainties of the textual transmission. But the corpus that has come down to us provides ample evidence of a powerfully coherent poetical and mystical imagination.

For Bullhe Shah, as for so many Sufis, the primary reason for creation was God's desire to be loved, and the primal compact between God and man meant both man's recognition of God as the lord of his devotion and the special presence of the divine within man as the noblest of God's creatures. A particular role is accorded to the prophet Muhammad, whose other name, Ahmad, symbolizes his intimate connection with Ahad, or God the One.

His mystical perception of the unity of all things in the divine is not merely intellectual. It is a dynamic process pursued through love, the source of both man's greatest delights and his most acute emotional suffering.

Appealing at several levels to so many of the deepest human aspirations, to a universal understanding of the meaning of human existence in a divine world, Bullhe Shah's assimilation of many diverse elements into his poetic expression of the philosophy of the unity of being makes him an outstanding interpreter of the transcendent, not just for Panjabis but for us all.

SUFI LYRICS

1

I am not a Hindu, nor a Muslim. I have forsaken pride
    and become unsullied.[6]
I am not a Sunni, nor a Shia. I have adopted the path of
    peace toward all.[7]
I am not hungry, nor am I full. I am not naked, nor am
    I covered.
I do not weep, nor do I laugh. I am not ruined, nor do
    I flourish.

I am not a sinner, nor am I virtuous. I do not know about
the path of sin and merit.

Bullhe Shah, the mind that is fixed on God leaves behind
the duality of Hindu and Turk.[8]

2

Now, love, you have come to us. You have come and we
are happy to see you.

You had Ibrahim thrown onto the pyre.[9] You had
Zakariya's head sawn.[10] You had Yusuf hawked from
stall to stall.[11] Tell us what you have brought for us.

You had the pigs grazed by Shaikh Sanaan.[12] You had
Shams hanged upside down and flayed.[13] You had
Mansur put up on the gallows.[14] Now you have
determinedly attacked me.

The house that you have visited has been on fire and
turned into a heap of ashes. Only when the ash flies
away are you satisfied. Tell us what you have set your
heart on.

Bullha, for the sake of the lord, let us make the body the
furnace, the mind the anvil, and love the hammer to
beat the iron of the heart that is melted in the fire.

3

Who are you hiding yourself from now?

Sometimes as a mullah you give the call to prayer,
sometimes you tell of religious practice and duty.
Sometimes you utter appeals to Ram, sometimes you
put the *tilak* on your forehead.[15]

This "I" may be mine or yours, but in the end it is a heap
    of ashes. This heap has been surrounded by the
    beloved, and it is set to dance.

Sometimes you will put on a nose ring and topknot,
    sometimes you will put on a costume and dress up.
    Sometimes you will come as Adam and Eve. Can you
    ever be mistaken, even by me?

You set up your camp outside in plain view, and it is you
    who beat the drum with a loud beat. You made
    yourself known to the world; then you raced to the
    house of Abdullah.[16]

Whoever searches for you dies before he is dead.[17] Even
    after death he fears you, in case the dead are killed and
    slaughtered.

In Bindraban you take the cows to pasture.[18] You sound
    the conch when attacking Lanka.[19] You come as a hajji
    from Mecca. How amazingly your appearance
    is varied.

Mansur came to you; it is you who seized him and made
    him mount the gallows. He is my dear brother, born
    of the same father. Blood money for my brother
    should be paid.

You are in all guises, you appear to me everywhere. It is
    you who are the wine and you who drink it. You are
    the one who makes you taste yourself.

Now I will remain with you. I will not lose heart and run
    away. I will tell all your mysteries. Why am I not to be
    embraced?

How wonderful, the one so favored is indeed just like you.
It is a reliable tradition that salvation is to be attained
through your look of kindness.

If the garden is planted in the flames, you display yourself
from the fire pit. When Ahad is made from *alif*,[20] how
is the hidden revealed?

You are friend, God, lord, and master. It is you who are
your own devoted follower. It is you who are the
creation and the creator. It is you who causes good
deeds to be performed.

Sometimes you are a thief, sometimes a *qazi*, sometimes a
preacher who climbs into the pulpit, sometimes Tegh
Bahadur,[21] the warrior for faith. You are the one who
causes your army to attack.

It is you who had Yusuf imprisoned, you who had Yunus
swallowed by the fish,[22] you who put the worms into
Ayub the patient,[23] then caused him to ascend the
throne.

If you taught the lesson of the word *man*,[24] then you hid
yourself well. You made the heart embrace the
fourteen spheres.[25] Thus this lengthy debate is
created.

Bullha, you are clearly recognized; lord, you are
apprehended through every form. Here you come,
here you go. Now you cannot be mistaken by me.

4

Now I have seen the fair beloved, whose beauty is always
in such demand.

When Ahad alone existed, no divine glory was manifest.
There was no Lord or Prophet or Allah, no Almighty,
no all-powerful God.

He was without parallel or analogy, without likeness or
comparison. There was no spectacle or model; now
there are thousands of things of all kinds.

The beloved came to put on various clothes; he called
himself Adam. From Ahad he turned himself into
Ahmad and came as the leader of the prophets.[26]

He said *Let it be* and caused *and it was* to be said, making
form from formlessness.[27] He mingled the *mīm* into
Ahad, and created this vast expanse.

I abandon the mosque, I abandon the idol temple. I do not
keep Hindu fasts, nor do I observe Ramadan. I have
forgotten ablutions and prayers with two
prostrations.[28] I sacrifice my life to you.

Saints and prophets are his slaves. Men and angels
prostrate themselves to him, laying their heads at his
feet. He is the greatest overlord of all.

No one who wishes to see him can do so without an
intermediary. If Shah Inayat reveals the secret, then
all mysteries are solved.

5

Now who can recognize me? Now I have become
something else.[29]

The guide taught me this lesson. There is no coming or
going of the other there. The absolute being displays
his beauty. Divine unity has created confusion.

Infinite at first, the beloved appears as manifest and
hidden. I have no name or mark anymore; all dispute
and confusion are ended.
When the beloved displays his beauty, drunken fakirs
become intoxicated. Now that I have observed the
graceful movement of the wild geese,[30] Bullha, I have
forgotten the motion of the crows.

6

I will play Holi, after saying *bismillāh*.[31]
I wear the name of the Prophet as my jewel, and the words
but God as my pendant.[32] He is the one who operates
this colorful show, from which the lesson of
annihilation in God is learned.[33]
When the beloved said, *Am I not your lord?*[34] the girls all
removed their veils. With the words *They said, "Yes,"*
they said, *There is no god but God.*
He played the flute of *We are nearer,*[35] and called out
Whoever has known himself.[36] *Then there is the face
of God* was loudly proclaimed in the court of God's
Apostle.[37]
I will humbly fold my hands and fall at his feet, and in my
helplessness I will entreat him. As my Holi offering, I
will fill my lap with the light of Muhammad, *may
God's blessing be upon him.*[38]
I will make *Then remember me* my Holi, and I will delight
my beloved with *And be thankful to me.*[39] Such is the
beloved to whom I am sacrificed, *glory be to God.*[40]
The syringe[41] was filled with *the dye of God*[42] and was
squirted on the face of *God the eternal.*[43] The light of

the Prophet proceeded from God, the light of
Muhammad, *may God's blessing be upon him*. Bullha,
the fame of the lord is loudly proclaimed: *There is no
god but God.*

7

Spin, my girl, do not idle. Take off your ball of yarn and
place it in the basket.

If you spin rolls and rolls of yarn, you will never wander
naked. If for a hundred years you do not spin, the crow
will swoop and attack you, my girl.

If you spend your days in obliviousness, if you do not spin
and accumulate something, then without any virtues
when your lord is beside you, how will you be saved,
my girl?

Your parents have tied your knots,[44] but you have still not
become aware. The days are few, but you have wasted
them in enjoyment. You will not return to your
parents' home, my girl.

If you go without a dowry, you will not please anyone.
How will you delight your lord when you get there?
Take some guidance from the fakirs, my girl.

Your companions have had their dowry clothes dyed and
are wearing their red outfits. Why have you gone the
wrong way? When you get there, you will realize the
true state of things, my girl.

Bullha, if the lord comes home, your bangles and anklets
all look fine. If you possess good qualities, he will
embrace you. Otherwise you will weep tears of blood,
my girl.

8

Will you ever call me your own?[45]

I am without merit; what virtuous action have I
performed? My body is the beloved, my heart is the
beloved. It is the beloved who is my life. Will you
come to me as beloved to beloved?

As the transitory, I make myself distant. As the enduring, I
make myself ever-present. If like Mansur I make
things very clear, will you seize me and make me
mount the gallows?

I am awake, but the whole world is asleep. When it opens
its eyes, it gets up and weeps. Intoxication is the only
thing that works. Will you ever make me drunk on
Am I not?

When you became unstruck,[46] you set your two eyes at
them. Hundreds of thousands laid down their severed
heads before you, and the ocean billowed with waves
of delight. Will you make the river of my blood flow?

Does any lover sleep peacefully? We have wept copiously
and bathed our face in tears. Is it magic or a spell that
you will use to turn this suffering into pleasure?

Say, what secret will love ponder? Then what will happen
when it decides? When the head has been sacrificed
on the gallows, will you later bang the drum?

I have made my heart a kebab. I have turned the liquor of
my eyes into wine, my veins into strings, and my bones
into a rebeck. What will you call this religion?

What is the point of torment? Deal in what pleases the
heart. Who is going to be given this world and the
next? Will you show me a vision of yourself?

Your vision has come and set me on fire. My two eyes have
    created a downpour. Daily you have come as Inayat.
    Is this how you will make yourself known?
Bullha, when you go to look at the lord, you will make
    these eyes see properly. It is then that you will obtain a
    true vision of him. Will you return home as Shah
    Inayat?

9

Do come someday and meet this wretch who is oppressed
    by separation.
If you fell in love, you would shriek, "Ah, ah!" What do
    you know of another's pain?
If anyone wants to purchase love, he should first give his
    head as a down payment.
The girls who have acted well have all passed over in turn.
    It is for the beloved to protect our honor.
Currents of pain and waves of cruelty surround this
    wretch, who has been sucked into the bottom of
    a whirlpool.[47]
I have left my parents and forgotten my girlfriends. I am
    sacrificed to the lord, to whom I appeal for justice.
Bullha, I am exhausted by my love for the lord, who has
    cast me into the whirlpool.

10

Do[48] come someday and meet me,[49] my beloved friend.
    My head is sacrificed to the roads on which you travel.

The *koil* flies up in the gardens and cries out, exhaling her burning pain.[50] I am wretched, my dark beloved has forgotten me.

Bullha, one day the lord will come home, and he will extinguish the fire that blazes within me. My head is sacrificed to the roads on which he travels.[51]

11

Sometime do turn back your reins, my love. My head is offered to the roads on which you travel.

Freshly washed and bathed, I have been left here. Some knot has settled in my lover's heart. Did I say something inappropriate?

Bullha, one day the lord will come home. He will extinguish the fire that blazes within me, whose pains are ready to devour me.

12

Why does the yellow *revaṛī* fight with the *patāsā*?[52]

The *laḍḍū* made with sesame seeds has arrested the *jalebī*. The *kand* has run in fear from the sugar and fought with the *misrī*. The crow has started killing the hawk, and the donkey's cheek is red.

The millionaires seek justice, and issue a summons on the salt.[53] The *gulgalās* have made a plan and wounded the *pāpaṛ*. The sheep have attacked the leopards and destroyed them, and the wolves are in a sorry state.

The *guṛ* and the *laḍḍū* have got angry and complained against the *peṛās*. The *canā dāl* said to the *barfī*, "You

are my slave girl." The rabbits attack and dance upon
the lions, and have a merry time.

The *shakar khand* says to the *misrī,* "Look how clean I
am." The *cirvās* and *canās* have started fighting with
the *badānās.* The rats nibble the cat's ears in great
delight.

Now what can Bullhe Shah say? Everyone you can see is
fighting. Kicking and pulling each other's hair, no one
holds another back. Behold the arrival of the day of
doom, with Dajjal on his donkey.[54]

13

Pay attention to your spinning, my girl.

Your mother is always admonishing you: Daughter, why
are you idly wandering about, you lazy thing? Do not
destroy your honor and reputation, daughter. Do have
some sense, you ignorant girl.

You got your spinning wheel for nothing. You did not have
to use any of your own money on it. You have not
realized the value of hard work, when the work has
proved easy, my girl.

The spinning wheel was made for you. Do not be so keen
to play. You are not going to be growing up anymore,
so come to your senses, you ignorant girl.

Your spinning wheel is brightly colored; the whole clan is
envious of it. Work as hard as you can and do well in
the house, my girl.

This spinning wheel has a high price, but what do you
know of its value, you peasant? You look down at

everyone as you strut about filled with arrogance,
being proud of your status, my girl.

I stand with arms outstretched and cry: Will you ever
come to your senses, you heedless one? No carpenter
is ever going to make you another spinning wheel like
this one, my girl.

Why have you spoiled this spinning wheel? Why have you
let it lie in the dust? Ever since you have had it, you
have never come to set it up, my girl.

I am always telling this half-witted, simple, mad, and
crazy girl: When you are all alone and bad times come,
your soul will cry "Alas, alas," my girl.

From the outset you have been without anything to live by.
You have not spun cotton rolls from the bunches of
yarn. Why do you go around now looking sad, and
what are you so proud of, my girl?

You do not set the spindle straight, nor do you set up the
connecting string and the driving band. Why do you
keep packing the spinning wheel away all the time?
You are bringing about your own ruin, my girl.

Set the twisted spindle straight, and quickly set up the
connecting string. Keep it moving naturally; do not
do anything stupid, my girl.

Today there is a fresh lot of raw cotton in the house, my
girl. Quickly start to roll it, my girl. Once it is rolled,
go to get it carded, my girl. You will not get to return
to it tomorrow, my girl.

When you bring the carded cotton, you will put the cotton
rolls on the wheel with your friends. Then you will be

the one who is popular throughout the whole world,
    my girl.

All the girls who are your companions have spun their
    cotton rolls.[55] As you sit there, they come for you,
    asking: Why are you sitting in such a daze, my girl?

Light a lamp beside you. Keep spinning and putting the
    hanks in the basket. Let night pass before your eyes,
    and do not take things easy, my girl.

You get just a few days to lord it in your father's house,
    my girl. Do not spend your time playing about, my
    girl. Do not remain idle but do something, my girl.
    Do not ruin your family, my girl.

Do not spend the night asleep. You are not going to come
    back a second time. You are not going to sit in this
    company again among your age-mates, my girl.

You are not going to remain in your father's house forever.
    You are not going to sit beside your dear mother. In
    the end you must endure separation from them, and
    you will come under the authority of your husband's
    mother and sisters, my girl.

Spin, and have it spun. Have the thread woven in the warp.
    Have your dowry clothes dyed; then you will be
    respected, my girl.

When you go to that house of strangers, you will never
    return from there again. When you arrive there, you
    will be sorry. Get your things ready in advance, my
    girl.

Today you have so much work to do, my girl. Why have
    you become so unconcerned, my girl? What will you

do at that moment, when the guests come to the
house, my girl?

When all your girlfriends leave, they will certainly not
come there again. They will never come to set up their
spinning wheels. Your spinning party will be deserted,
my girl.

Do not be proud of your beauty and youth. Travelers do
not remain in a foreign country. No name or mark of
this false and transitory world will remain, my girl.

A difficult time will come. All your family and kin will flee.
The one who will come to your aid and get you across
is Bullha's sovereign,[56] my girl.

14

Why do you sit in concealment and peep out? Who are you
veiling yourself from?

You came for the sake of love, turning yourself into
someone to love. You placed the veil of *mīm* over your
face, and from Ahad you made your name Ahmad.[57]
The royal umbrella of *If it were not for you* sways over
your head.[58]

You yourself are all things, so why do you say you are
separate? You have come as your own spectacle,
interposing the dividing line of earthliness.[59]

Apart from you, who else is there? Why have you created
this futile dispute? You saw a great darkness; now you
call yourself yourself.

Sometimes you are a Turk, sometimes a Syrian,[60]
sometimes the master, sometimes the slave. You

yourself embrace entirety, irrespective of the
   appearance of things being false or true.
The body that is filled with the passion of love loses self
      and consciousness. How can someone who has drunk
      from the cupbearer's goblet remain silent?[61]
You were the one who rushed at us; when did you ever
      remain hidden? You have come as Shah Inayat. Now
      keep your eyes fixed on us.
Bullhe Shah, make your body a furnace, burn your bones
      in the fire, and turn your body into dust. Make this
      love and desire your food for the journey; this is how
      to taste this wine.

15

Why do you dispute, why do you dispute with us over
      another's sin?[62]
You were the one who wrote *You do not move*.[63] So who are
      you causing to be hanged?
There was the law and the followers of the Qur'an, but we
      were called before they were.
Am I not your lord?[64] was revealed, and up went the loud
      cry *They said, "Yes."*
When *Let it be, and it was* was proclaimed, we too were
      there.[65]
Inflicting ecstasy, he has driven us mad; otherwise we
      should have retained our original nature.

16

Whom do you describe as infinite? You dwell in every
color.

You are the one who said *Let it be,* and caused *as it was* to be
said.[66] Who came but you? From love you created the
manifest world, where you dwell as your lover.[67]

Ask Adam this: Who brought him, where did he come
from, and where does he go? Whom did he deal with
there, when he ate the grain and ran away?[68]

You are the one who listens and the one who tells. You are
the one who sings and the one who plays. You made
the melody of the word sound from his hand, then as
the ignorant one you fled.[69]

Unity is yours and you are the one who makes it
understood. You play the string of *I am God.*[70] You
made Mansur mount the gallows, while you stood
around and laughed.[71]

Like Sikandar coming to Nushaba,[72] you come as the
Apostle with the scriptures. As Yusuf in her dreams,[73]
you steal the heart of Zulaikha.

Now you are a Greek, now you are an African, now you are
a European in a hat. Now you are a hashish addict in
the tavern, now you live comfortably as a respectable
married couple.

Bullha, Shah Inayat is a master mystic, he is the lord of my
heart. I am iron and he is the philosopher's stone.[74]
You snatch hold of me and make us touch.

17

What is he doing, what is he doing? Someone should ask
what the beloved is doing.

Those who live happily together in one house do not need
a screen between them.

He performs the prayer in the mosque, he goes into the
idol temple.

There is just one of him and many hundreds of thousands
of houses, but he is the master of every house.

Wherever I look, there is only him. He keeps company
with everyone.

He created Moses and Pharaoh.[75] Why does he turn
himself into two and fight?

Present and seeing, only he exists everywhere. Who does
the informer seize?

How can I tell such a sensitive secret? I cannot utter it, nor
can I bear it.

On this side and that side there is only him. He is the
master and the slave.

The river of unity is true. Everyone can be seen swimming
there.

Bullha, love for the lord is a young tiger. It drinks blood
and it eats flesh.

18

What is this nonchalance he practices?

He said *Let it be* and made them say *and it was.*[76] The
hidden proceeded to the manifest. He fashioned form
from formlessness and set up a complex game.

At the moment he spoke of the hidden secret, he
removed the veil from his face.[77] Now why does he
conceal himself from us? True reality has entered
everything.

We have honored the sons of Adam,[78] for no one like you has
been made. Such is the glory that goes with greatness;
the drum was properly beaten.[79]

He is the one who acts nonchalantly, he is the one who is
afraid of himself. He is present in every house, while
people roam in confusion.

He displayed his charms and he became mad. He became
Laila to make Majnun fall in love.[80] He was the one
who wept, he was the one who wailed. What a
wonderful kind of love he made.

You yourself are the beloved and the girls. All reason and
logic have vanished. Bullha, the lord has taken away
joys; why does he now inflict separation?

19

What do I know of anyone, my friend, what do I know
of anyone?

Whoever speaks and moves inside us is our essential
being. I have become identical with the one I fell in
love with.

Get rid of your white shawl, girl, and put on the fakirs'
blanket. The white shawl will get covered with stains,
but there is no stain on the blanket.[81]

I recognized *alif,*[82] I recognized *be,* then *te* began my
scriptural recitation. I recognized *sīn,*[83] I recognized
shīn, then I became sincere and patient.

"Coo, coo," said the turtledove, with your ring around its
    neck.[84] Its cooing never stops. It was still busy cooing
    when it died.

Whatever he does, it is God's will; what can anyone do by
    himself? I am grateful for whatever fate is written on
    my forehead.

The lover is the goat and the beloved is the butcher. Saying
    "Me, me,"[85] it is slaughtered. The more it says "Me,
    me," the deader it is.

Bullha, the lord in his grace gave me the wine of passion.[86]
    It is good that we have been set free from distant
    separation and that you have come near and found us.

20

With those who are cruel, what love is possible? My eyes
    are weeping bitterly.

The cruel ones abandoned us and went away, transfixing
    our breast with the spear of separation and removing
    the life from our body. This is what those murderers
    did.

What trust can be placed in the cruel, who do not have an
    ounce of fear in their hearts? The death of birds is a
    joke to peasants; afterward they laugh and clap their
    hands.

They said they would come but did not, forgetting all their
    promises of coming. I wander lost but have fixed my
    eyes on them. How will I get to see those robber
    traders?

Bullhe Shah did a deal, he drank the cup filled with the
poison of love. He got no profit and no loss; his bundle
of pains and sorrows is heavy.

21

What are these false promises you offer? Meet me for just
a couple of moments.

You live near but do not tell me the place. In which
direction should I look for you? It is you who peep out
as Ahmad. When I look, you are no longer there.

You promised when you went, but you have not returned.
Flames blaze in my breast. Living happily in the same
house, where else should I cry out to you?[87]

Go, traveler, and deliver my message. How can you hide in
the cover of the heart? In the name of God, do not be
hostile. Do not make me long to see your face.

Bullha, what has the lord done to me? In the middle of the
night I sing your praises. Everyone fears the wild river
glades, but that is where I search most happily.

22

Who has come dressed up, my girl?[88] Ask him straight,
my girl.

A crook is in his hand and a black blanket on his shoulders;
light dwells in the eyes. He is not a herdsman but a
man of wisdom. Get him to sit beside you and
question him, my girl.

Do not call him a menial herdsman.[89] He is not devoid of
secret purpose. Separated since the first night,[90] he
has come to search, my girl.

He is no one's menial herdsman, nor does he take the least
 pleasure in buffaloes. He has no desire for milk or
 yogurt, nor does he feel hunger or thirst, my girl.
Bullha, the lord sits hidden in concealment. He does not
 reveal the secret or speak with his mouth. My father
 seeks a bridegroom from the Kheras,[91] but my
 bridegroom is by my side, my girl.

23

Those made of dust must mingle with the dust. Force and
 might are of no avail.
Those who have gone have gone, they have not returned,
 my dear beloved friends. They could not bear to live
 without me, so now why have they forgotten us?
 There is no awareness in the grave, so why this
 anguished thrashing about?[92]
Our memory and love for them do not leave us, and we
 cannot stop sobbing. We have passed far beyond the
 dead, even as we sit among the living. Today or
 tomorrow we shall experience the great distress of
 departure.
The constables pursued us there, so we came here. We do
 not get to stay here; where will we move in the future?
 We are headed for the fate that befell those who went
 before us.
Bullha, no one gets to stay here. They departed weeping
 and beating their breasts. It is only his name that is
 our provision for the journey, we carry no other
 money. I am a dream, the whole world is a dream,
 and my father's people are a dream.

10.

Selections from *Selected Ghazals and Other Poems*

by Mir Taqi Mir

Translated from Urdu
by Shamsur Rahman Faruqi

Muhammad Taqi, who later earned lasting renown as the great Urdu poet Mir Taqi Mir, or Muhammad Taqi Mir—or just Mir—was born in Agra (better known at that time as Akbarabad) in September 1723. He died in Lucknow on September 10, 1810.[1] He compiled his first poetry collection (*divan*) some time in the early 1750s, certainly before 1752. He wrote both Persian and Urdu poetry and was prolific in all the popular genres. His *Kulliyāt* (Collected Poems) was published by the College of Fort William in 1811, setting perhaps the final seal of authority on his position as the major poet of the time.

In Urdu love poetry of the eighteenth century, both the speaker and beloved were a notion or ideal, as in the poetic conventions of the popular Persian ghazals in the *sabk-e hindi*, or "Indian style," freed from the demands of "reality." Ghazals were intended for recitation and their key theme was love. The core function of love was to soften the heart, to make it receptive to more pain, which ultimately made the human heart receptive to the divine light. Pain, and things that caused pain, had a positive value. The lover's place was to suffer; the beloved's function was to inflict suffering. This was a Sufi formulation, but it was regularly taken by the ghazal poet to be true in the ghazal universe.

The world of the ghazal is one where the outsider is the hero, where nonconformism is the creed, and where prosperity is poverty.

The lover-protagonist and the beloved-object both live in a world of extremes: supreme beauty, supreme cruelty, supreme devotion—all things are at their best, or worst, in this world. It reverberates throughout with the terror and the ecstasy of dying. Death, in spite of all its uncertainty and unfamiliarity, is an achievement, a respite, a transition. All this is often expressed with the subtlest of wordplay, in the most vigorously metaphorical language, and, occasionally, with extremely vivid but generally noncarnal realizations of the beloved's body.

The beloved's gender in the premodern ghazal can be a trouble-some issue for readers. In Urdu a convention developed in the late seventeenth century, contrary to the convention in nearly all South Asian poetry, to talk of the beloved as a male. In this edition, the beloved's gender is translated as female, unless the context is clearly incompatible with a female beloved, and a male beloved or God is clearly being talked about. The implications of the language of the poem are such that, by disregarding the surface differences of gen-der, one can often imagine the beloved to be God, or any ideal being, or a woman or a man or a boy.

The ambiguity of the atmosphere in this poetry can permit the "sacred" interpretation as often as not. Mir is rather an exception in being more than usually involved in worldly experience, but his poetry is full of Sufi themes as well.

Mir also wrote *masnavi,* narrative or philosophical poems in rhyming couplets. Among them is "Scolding the Rains," a poem about a ruinous storm, that is unique in the Urdu language, and perhaps in any language: it is comic, and not eschewing a bit of salacious salt.

Mir's poetry abounds in bawdiness, the pain and enjoyment of life, instances of homosexuality, Sufi themes, close and wise observation of the world, and insistence on man's dignity. His achievement, rarely equaled and never surpassed, is that many of his ghazal verses are brimming with emotional affect and, at first glance, do not seem to be *saying* much. An expert or close reader would, however, soon find that more has been said in the poem than is apparent on the surface.

GHAZALS

1

What can I tell you, and how, about the reality of love?
For those who know truth, love is God.

If your heart is stuck somewhere in love, well, all interest
    in life is gone for you.
Death is the name that people use lovingly for love.

Sorry, no remedy, no regimen can have any effect at all.
The cure for the ache of love is love.

It drowned me in an ocean of pain, truly.
I had believed that love was a friend—and a good
    swimmer.

There is no place empty of love.
It fills all space from the human heart to the seat of the
    almighty.

You think Farhad the mountain cutter carved right
    through the rocky ridge?
Well, actually it was love exerting its might, and just using
    him as a smoke screen.

Oh, I do admire those who do the business of love!
The kinds of love, states of love that they have managed to
    find are numberless.

Were there any who reached their purpose without love?
Love is what one longs for, love—the object of existence.

Well, Mir, one has no choice in the matter but to die for
    the beautiful ones.
Do not do love. Love is a bad one, a calamity in fact.

2

Quite often, my good man, people ask: Tell us, what is
    love?
Some say it is God's own secret while others declare it is
    God.

Love's glory is always high, but its tasks and actions are
    wondrous.
It sometimes courses through the heart and the mind;
    sometimes it is different—or indifferent to all.

Loving the young softwood trees of the garden of love is
    tough business.
Love is a penalty and pain, really—if one doesn't fall
    unconscious breathing in the fragrance of that apple,
    the rounded chin.[2]

You there! Beware of love and keep away. It causes
    terrible, dire suffering.
Love is pain and grief and hardship, a bane and pest of the
    spirit—a fiend in fact.

One who loves someone contrary to his temperament,
    Mir, will drink bitter drafts.
And if one finds a lover who is not contrary? Loving then is
    a pleasure, pure enjoyment.

3

The earth, according to lovers, is cold, mere dust, but it's
    where love has its dwelling place.
And the sky? It is the dust that floats around on the
    highway of love.

The weak and wan Majnun is popular, and not only in the
    cities.
Love commands goodwill and high regard also among the
    wild dwellers in the wilderness.

How great were the people of the true path whose houses
    were given over to emptiness and waste!
In a word, the city of love has always been a wasteland.[3]

To suffer sorrows mutely makes the heart's wounds
    chronic, even cancerous, and yet
the holder of the secret of love does not open his heart to
    weeping.

Poor Mir, he wastes himself at the first stage of loving,
    though in fact he is
a wanderer far and wide in the valley of love, which preys
    on madness and hunts it down.

4

Although you never do so, yet I beg you, please look at me
    and look—
I long for you to turn toward me and look.

Love exposes me to hardship in such quantity and variety
that you too would cast an eye and look!

Perspiration on her face glows
like the dew on the rose, just look.

Each scratch on my forehead became a gash.
It's the artwork of loving fingernails—just take a look.

I longed for smiling lips.
Instead I was given eyes that weep. Do you see?

It tugs at the heart, even the color has fled.
Stay here another night, until it becomes morning, and
    see.[4]

The heart prepares to defy love.
A mere drop of blood, and such nerve, just see!

I am near to dying,
about to leave for a faraway place, if you would just reflect
    a moment and look.

Mir, I too have any number of delightful graces.
I am worth a glance—if you would just consider and look.

5

Heartsick I passed through a garden yesterday.
The roses were about to say, "So, how are you?" but I
    didn't even look at them.

The morning breeze woke you from slumber.
You're angry at me, but did I do it?

I walked straight into the edge of your sword.
So what could I do? I used my battered heart as shield.

Short sword in hand and eyes bloodred from drink:
you mischief maker, you cut such an elegantly forbidding
    figure that I avoided facing you.

The dirt of the road trampled underfoot day and night
    can't compare with my state.
What more can I say, except that that was how I lived my
    life?

My sharp fingernails made short work of both my heart
    and liver.
It was indeed artistic, the way I nightly scratched at my
    breast.

Only such as I can put those lips to work the way I did.
I made my home in her eyes in no more than a twinkling or
    two of the eye.

It was like someone departing the world with unfulfilled
    longings in tow.
That was how I left the street of the person who stole my
    heart.

Well, yesterday I somehow managed to resist the cruel one
    who thirsted for my blood.
If you're a fair judge you'll see it was no mean feat of valor.

Very often, ah Mir, I remember and sing her praises:
    "What long hair! What a face!"
In fact, I've now made it my custom to repeat those words,
    night and day, like a pious man telling his beads.

6

My beloved rode out from the city and the outskirts are
    thick with dust today.
Bird and beast from the bush are hers, she'll shoot only
    sharp arrows today.

How elegant her face that blazes when she's drunk!
She drank a few cups and blossomed—springtime upon
　　that newly bloomed rose today.

The ocean of her loveliness swells and rises high in clash
　　and tumult.
Let desire's eye roam how far it may; it is hugs and kisses
　　through and through, today.
Her eyes reddening, her head dizzy,
she drank and then went to bed, and is hungover in the
　　morning, asking for more today.

You took the trouble to come calling at a fakir's home. So
　　do me a favor, and kindly sit here a while.
What do I possess but life? I offer it at your feet today.

Don't ask how much it writhed and throbbed in my side
　　until twilight yesterday.
Well, by and by, somehow, my heart became somewhat
　　stable today.

Don't miss out on this chance: bring your heart—most
　　valuable merchandise—there and nowhere else.
There's a mighty kingdom of Hindu boys ruling in
　　Hindustan today.[5]

I opened my eyes wide to see and found her just like a rose
　　branch.

She seemed absorbed in their radiant appearance, so
    mixed up as she was in those colors and flowers today.

Love's galvanism will draw Laila's howdah where it will:
the reins of her camel are in Majnun's hands today.

She didn't take off in the morning the flower garland she
    wore last night, Mir.
Was it because the rose's charm stubbornly clung to her
    neck like a necklace's beads today?

7

Is it the bulbul that's in the cage, shorn of wings and
    feathers? Or is it I?
Does the rose have a heart in tatters, or do I?

Does the sun rise every morning in such radiant splendor,
    or do you?
Does the morning dew have eyes suffused with tears,
    or do I?

Well, if I survive, I will expose the bulbul's boast.
In the dry season when the rose departs, will he embrace
    death, or will I?

Look, here's your sword, here the basin to receive my
    head.
Here am I—does anyone else play so lightly with his life
    as I?

I am wordless while you rain down sword strokes on me.
Would anyone else in the world let such things pass other
    than I?

What else can I say of my ruination in my search for her?
Did the breeze ever wander homeless so much from place
    to place as I?

I promptly came to know when you were trapped
    somewhere,
dear heart. Who else keeps so informed a vigil over you
    as I?

I live and weep with my heart in shreds, oh Mir!
Have you ever heard of anyone else who chopped his heart
    to mincemeat but I?

8

Things went the way man liked, and did you see what he
    did then?
He made the sky—his eternal enemy—run around like a
    lackey, measuring the length and breadth of the earth!
The sky goes round and round in his service all the time.
Night came on when day ended.
The moon, the sun, clouds, the wind
roam far and away, wander crazy for him.
How much digging, how much ploughing before
things of all kinds and hues could be produced and
    procured for him!

He was designated the most preferred of all.
God's benevolence elevated his status.
How astonishing to behold his ways—
self-indulgent, self-regarding, self-opinionated.
Among the modes of prostration for giving thanks it was
    best for him
to ceaselessly rub his forehead on the ground.
So what did he do? Did his stubborn temperament
let him bend his head even once if at all?
Oh my God, Mir! That handful of dirt, not worth a trifle—
where did it learn such arrogance, such contumacy?

9

I came like a fakir, made a beggar's call, departed.
Dear child, I offer a blessing: may you always be happy. I
    depart.[6]

Do you remember? I declared I won't live without you.
So I now redeem that vow. I depart.

Well, actually it wasn't fated that I survive.
So, having received all the treatment I could, I depart.

Such causes befell in the end
that, having no choice, and with my soul burnt to ashes, I
    depart.

God! What is that thing for which
I detach my heart from all other things, and depart?

I would at least cast a despairing eye on you
but you even veiled your face from me, and now you
      depart.

Oh, how much I longed to set foot in your street!
So now bathed in my own blood I depart.

Catching sight of you just once, a mere glimpse, caused my
      senses to reel.
You took me away from myself, and then you depart.

My forehead worn down by continual prostration—
having fulfilled my duty as a servant, I depart.

Stony idol of beauty, I adored you to the utmost,
established you as the true God in everyone's regard, and
      now I depart.

It was the way the flowers die and fall from the branch
      where they were born.
I came into this garden called the world, and now I depart.

Thank God, I didn't have to face the sorrow of my friends'
      deaths.
It was I who etched my grief upon them, and now I depart.

Bound with the chains of the worry-filled practice of
      making *ghazals,* my life passed.

And now, having raised that art to such greatness, I
    depart.

What should I say in reply, oh Mir, were someone to ask
    me,
what did you do here in this world now that you depart?

10

Just look, does it rise from the heart or from the soul?
It's something like smoke but from where does it arise?

Is it a burnt heart that lies buried in the sky?
A flame arises there at every break of dawn.

Never, never go away from the heart's quarter.
Did anyone ever leave such an excellent dwelling place?

Every time my wailing rises up
a tumultuous clamor arises in the sky.

In whatever spot her bold and seductive eye strikes
a tumult of calamities arises.

Fiery, passionate voice: shouldn't you look to your own
    house?
There's something, something like smoke, that arises from
    your house.

You think anybody ever would let him settle down again,
the one who once rose from your doorstep?

I left someone's street—ah, it was just the way
one leaves this world.

Love is a stone with a mighty heft, oh Mir!
Hoisting it will never be possible for a frail man like you.

11

If Mir keeps on wailing so loud
how can his neighbor not lose sleep?

I who shed tears so profuse now depart this world,
a weeper for whom the clouds will weep year after year.

Dear counselor, it's my avocation to weep often.[7]
How long will you keep washing away the tears from my
    face?

Stop, tears, stop! Don't you have eyes to see?
Will you go on flooding the world forever?

My heart raises a lament so poignant and powerful
that even the caravan's loud bell would lose its senses
    upon hearing it.[8]

Well, so be it, you can abuse my rivals as much as you like.
You'll get like for like if you do it with me.

Mir, enough. Wipe the tears from your lashes.
How long will you keep on stringing those pearls?

12

My sorrow remained as long as the breath of life remained
    in me.
I grieved deeply over the loss of my heart.

Your beauty, young man, drew the world's attention.
And a world of beauty remained even when the down
    appeared upon your face.

I wept my heart out, but my tears couldn't reach even the
    hem of my tunic.
The heart, a mere drop of blood, clotted on my eyelashes.

I heard that Laila's tent was black.
Perhaps they lamented in mourning for Majnun there?[9]

Friends, don't be deceived by the pious man's formal
    garment, the sort donned by the hajji.
True, he was in the Kaaba but he remained a total stranger,
    a person before whom the mysteries must veil
    themselves.

You undid your hair and revealed your face for only a
    moment,
but my heart's purposes were upended for a whole
    lifetime.

I heard vitriolic words from her lips all the time.
But the poison that dripped from her lips worked like the
    elixir of life for me.

The piece of paper on which was written the full and true
    account of my weeping
remained moist for a long, long time.

Mir, the morning of hoary old age now verges upon the
    evening.
Alas, you paid no mind and now but little of the day remains.

13

My existence is like a bubble's;
what seems to be life is rather like a mirage.

Can anyone at all express how delicate are her lips?
They're rather like the petal of a rose.[10]

Open your heart's eyes on that other world too.
What is found here is worth rather less than a dream.

I go to her door again and again
in a growing state of uncontrollable agitation.

The beauty mark between your brows
is rather like a selection dot between the two lines of a
    verse.[11]

I spoke a few words at her door, and at once she said: this
    voice
is surely like his, that home destroyer, that homeless
    fellow.

Is my heart being roasted by the fires of sorrow?
For quite some time there has been something rather like
    the scent of kebabs around here.

Just look, the cloud this time billows out
somewhat like my tear-filled eyes.

Those half-opened eyes, oh Mir,
are intoxicated themselves and they go to the head like
    wine.

SCOLDING THE RAINS THAT HAD BEEN PARTICULARLY HEAVY IN THE YEAR THE POEM WAS WRITTEN

How to describe the state of the rains this season?
Words have been swept away by the furious torrents.
The drops of rain don't stop falling this year.
The sky is like a sieve with water poured from above.
Dark and heavy rains fall ceaselessly, monotonously.
The sky pines for an eye to open.[12]
There is no moonrise, no sunrise,
and the stars, sunk by the rains, don't rise to the surface.
None open their mouths, but they talk of water.
The heavens just do not open an eye.
Since there's water right up to the sky,

the moon and the fish that supports the earth are now
   companions.
Everything from earth to sky is under water.
The streams of light that flow from the sun are now
   whirlpools.
Dry scrublands are verdant at this time.
The porcupine's quills have turned green.
How drunken, how besotted the black clouds
that keep rising from the lowlands!
The young boys have made up with the times: rather than
play by hiding things in dust heaps, they now sport in
   water.
The clouds discharge rain copiously,
and lands once desiccated have been shamed into
   becoming lakes.[13]
Don't be obtuse, my words are hardly turgid:
the ship of the heavens is about to sink in the rising water!
Rain and yet more rain has driven everyone half-mad.
Discourses, reputations—all are sunk in water.
What a deluge the rains have sent forth!
Even the heart's wounds must have dropsy, secreting
   water as they do.
Doors and terraces start to subside, not to rise again—
such is the fate of the city laid to waste by water.
My ceiling—a heap of earth for target practice; the
   raindrop—the point of an arrow.
Is it rain or a shower of arrows?
Bubbling and flooding over like the rivers—
the water outlets and drains are now seen to be flowing.

Is the raincloud God's mercy, or a throng of troubles?
The world is drowning in a flood of God's mercy!
The floods have taken off with the world.
It seems hardly more than a drawing writ on water.
Nothing, not gatherings or meetings with friends,
inhabits the city—nothing but wind and rain.
All the time, day and night, we see flashes.
Lightning has achieved maximum brightness these days.
Beware the blows and bruises when large raindrops fall.
Better to bury yourself under a shower of stones.
All of us learn the lesson of wonderment.
There's water in the ring-mirror's frame too.[14]
If any human beings are here, they hardly ever come out.
It's just water creatures one sees moving about.
Where are the dogs? All have drowned—
there are no dogs, only beavers everywhere.[15]
Don't ask, dear friend, about the expanse of the waters,
even bazaars are now flowing like waves.
All places of worship collapse and fall, one by one—
the pious, dry by temperament, are about to drown.
It was hazardous to stay around them,
immersed as they are in saintly thoughts in the mosques.
Well, the rain—it raineth every day,
but now everyone's ears run with pus.
The birds are under water; the squirrels too—
even the creatures of dry land are now *bahri*.[16]
The rainwater flows on so boldly
it is about to sink the whole world.
All creatures, whether in water or on dry land, are sodden.
Hot terror shrivels up all householders' spirits.

Poetry's meters are also waterlogged.[17]
Ghazal composing and singing have both floated away.
The quickness of the falling rain
has brought moisture even to the pearl's dry water.[18]
The crops have been killed off by water;
putrid and sour watermelon is the only vegetable there is.
The world is water, through and through.
The juicy fruits are dried out from fear.
The drunkards are drunk, ever so drunk.
Blind-drunk they dive and plunge in the water.
It's free and full enjoyment for those who wish to take a
    day out upon water.
Wine-ducks are all water birds now.[19]
All whores known for their frigid dryness
now have floods rising from their cunts.[20]
Their pants, sopping wet, are like gunny sacks.
The devastation spreads and flows in their vaginas.
The power of dark clouds is now so turbulent
that there is a deluge at every corner.
Did you ever see a flood's torrent down the side of the tall
    hills?
Now they seem like paupers begging for rains, bowl in
    hand.
The ebbs and flows reach up to the sky.
Every little lake has an ocean's fury now.
Black clouds on all sides wherever you look,
water is all there is to see.
Floods accompany our sight wherever it reaches.
It's an ocean as far as the eye can see.[21]
The water has risen right up to our heads.

Those with dry and barren brains have finally a wet tongue
    in their heads.
I am wondering how Khizr can keep body and soul
    together:
at the source of the Water of Life, the water is dead and
    putrid.
How can poor Mir describe the ferocious overflow of the
    rains?
Even his ink has turned to water.

NOTES

Foreword

1   Some readers may hear, in this assertion, an echo of Michael Cohen's 1992 essay, "On Reading 'Hamlet' for the First Time," in which he explores the implications of teaching or discussing literary texts, artistic masterpieces, or musical compositions (he cites, among others, Shakespeare's *Hamlet,* Leonardo da Vinci's *Mona Lisa,* and Beethoven's Ninth Symphony) that have assumed a legendary reputation for an audience that may not have had any firsthand experience of these works. Cohen's concern is with "unteaching" the context of received, often clichéd ideas surrounding such works, in the interests of reading them afresh, without preconceptions, in potentially overlooked detail and against the grain. By contrast, Ramanujan's concern is with embracing literary classics in the expansiveness of their shapeshifting presence and playful intertextuality, in contexts across media and domains of reception, which would allow for another kind of sophisticated, associative reading. See Michael Cohen, "On Reading *Hamlet* for the First Time," *College Literature: A Journal of Critical Literary Studies* 19, no. 1 (February 1992): 48–59.

2   A. K. Ramanujan, "Repetition in the *Mahābhārata,*" in *The Collected Essays of A. K. Ramanujan* ed. Vinay Dharwadker (New Delhi: Oxford University Press, 1999), 161.

3   A. K. Ramanujan, "Three Hundred *Rāmāyaṇa*s: Five Examples and Three Thoughts on Translation," in *The Collected Essays of A. K. Ramanujan,* 134.

4   This witticism is, in fact, a translation of a remark made in Yiddish in the course of a speech that Weinrich gave on January 5, 1945. See *YIVO Bleter* 25, no. 1 (January-February 1945).

5   Clifford Geertz, "Found in Translation: On the Social History of the Moral Imagination," in *Local Knowledge: Further Essays in Interpretive Anthropology* (New York: Basic Books, 1983), 54.

6   Italo Calvino, "Why Read the Classics?," in *Why Read the Classics?,* trans. Martin McLaughlin (London: Vintage, 2000), p. 8.

NOTES

Selections from the Therīgāthā

1   Translation slightly adapted from Peter Masefield, trans., *The Udāna Commentary (Paramatthadīpanīnāma Udānaṭṭhakathā)* by Dhammapāla, Sacred Books of the Buddhists 43 (Oxford: Pali Text Society, 1994), 2–3.

2   There is no single method or type of criteria that allows us to date the individual poems of the *Therīgāthā* with certainty, and scholars have tried to use doctrinal, metrical, and linguistic criteria to establish relative dating for individual poems in the anthology. Sometimes the various methods used for dating are not only inconclusive but yield results that are contradictory in the details. Still, as Norman says, when all the results are put together, "we may ... conclude that all the evidence supports the view that the verses collected together in the [*Therīgāthā*] were uttered over a period of about 300 years, from the end of the 6th century to the end of the 3rd century B.C." K. R. Norman, trans., *The Elders' Verses II Therīgāthā*, 2nd ed. (London: Pali Text Society, 2007), xxxi. See also Oskar Von Hinüber, *A Handbook of Pāli Literature* (Berlin: de Gruyter, 1996), 53; and Siegfried Lienhard, "Sur la structure poétique des Theratherīgāthā," *Journal Asiatique* 263 (1975): 375–396.

3   See verse 420 of *Saṃyutta-nikāya*, vol. I., ed. L. Feer (Oxford: Pali Text Society, 1884); Bhikkhu Bodhi, trans., *The Connected Discourses of the Buddha: A Translation of the* Saṃyutta Nikāya (Boston: Wisdom Publications, 2000), 1843–1852.

4   Therika was born in a rich Kshatriya family. She was given the name "Therika" because of her firm (*thferi*), peaceful body. She had already been married when the Buddha came to where she lived. She was drawn to the way of life that he taught just by seeing him. Later she was taught by Mahapajapati Gotami, the stepmother of the Buddha and prominent among the nuns of the *Therīgāthā*, and she wanted to become a renunciant. Therika's husband did not permit her to go forth, but she practiced what she had been taught as a laywoman until her husband could see the transformations in her. He brought her to Mahapajapati Gotami for ordination. After Therika was ordained, Mahapajapati Gotami brought her to the Buddha. After he taught her, he said this verse to her. When she heard the verse, Therika was enlightened. Therika repeated what the Buddha said, making the verse an expression of her own experience.

208

The rubric in the canonical *Therīgāthā* introduces the subject of this verse merely as "a certain unknown nun," Dhammapala takes the "therike" in the verse as her proper name [therīkā]; Norman takes it as descriptive diminutive and translates "little therī." K. R. Norman, trans., *The Elders' Verses II Therīgāthā*, 2nd ed. (London: Pali Text Society, 2007), 60.

5   Mutta was born in a wealthy Brahman family. She was ordained by Mahapajapati Gotami at the age of twenty and was very devoted to meditation. One day while Mutta was meditating, the Buddha sent a vision of himself to her and used it to speak this verse to her. When she was enlightened, she repeated the verse as her own. She repeated it again at the time of her death.

6   The demon that causes eclipses.

7   Punna was born in a wealthy family and was ordained by Mahapajapati Gotami. The Buddha sent a vision of himself to her and used it to speak this verse to her. The verse encouraged her to do what was necessary to become enlightened. She repeated the verse when she was enlightened to announce the achievement.

8   Tissa was born in the Sakya royal family, the same family as the Buddha's birth family. When she reached adulthood, she was one of the future Buddha's concubines. Later she joined Mahapajapati Gotami in renunciation. The Buddha sent a vision of himself to her and used it to speak this verse. She was enlightened from hearing this verse.

9   Dhammapala says that this Tissa's story is the same as the previous Tissa's; this is also the case for Dhira, Vira, Mitta, Bhadra, and Upasama, whose verses follow. William Pruitt, trans., *The Commentary on the Verses of the Therīs* (Oxford: Pali Text Society, 1999), 19–20. All were royal concubines of the future Buddha before he set forth on his quest for enlightenment. The Buddha spoke a verse to each of them through a radiant vision that he sent to each, except for Vira who received her verse from the Buddha himself. Each of these *therīs* was enlightened when she heard her verse from the Buddha, and each repeated the verse spoken by the Buddha to her to announce her achievement.

10   *Bhāvitindriyā*, with sense and cognitive faculties well-cultivated.

11   Mutta was the daughter of a poor Brahman. When she had reached puberty, her parents gave her in marriage to a hunched-back Brahman. Unhappy in her life with him, she received permission from her husband to become a nun. She used this verse in her own spir-

itual practices. If, in meditation, her mind wandered, she said this verse to restore her concentration. She repeated the verse again when she was enlightened.

12   Dhammadinna was born in a respectable family and then was married to a wealthy merchant. Her husband went to hear the Buddha and was transformed spiritually by that experience. As a result, he wanted to be celibate. After asking Dhammadinna's own wishes, he sent her to live among the Buddha's ordained female followers. After Dhammadinna was enlightened, she returned to where her husband lived and preached the Buddha's teaching to him. The Buddha later praised her as the best among the nuns in preaching the dhamma. She spoke this verse at the time of her enlightenment, as she reflected on the effort that she had made.

13   Dhammapala interprets "who is bound upstream" in a general sense of "up the stream of continued existence" (*saṃsārasoto*) and as one who has gone "up the stream of the path," and indicates that Dhammadinna is so spiritually advanced that she will not be reborn. Pruitt, *The Commentary on the Verses of the Therīs*, 31.

14   Dhammapala says that Visakha's story is the same as Dhira's. Pruitt, *The Commentary on the Verses of the Therīs*, 31. This would mean that she also was a concubine of the future Buddha's. She said this verse at the time of her enlightenment not only to announce her own achievement, but also to encourage others in their efforts.

15   Dhammapala says that her story is the same as Tissa's. Pruitt, *The Commentary on the Verses of the Therīs*, 32. The Buddha sent a vision to her. It looked as if he were seated in front of her, and it spoke this verse to her. At the end of the verse, she was enlightened.

16   The *dhātu* are the primary elements of all that exists, and a conventional set of them consists of earth, water, fire, and wind.

17   Dhammapala says that her story is the same as Tissa's. Pruitt, *The Commentary on the Verses of the Therīs*, 33. She too was born in the Sakya royal family and was a concubine of the future Buddha's. She went forth with Mahapajapati Gotami. The Buddha spoke this verse to her in a vision, and when he was finished she was enlightened. She then repeated the verse as an account of her own experience.

18   Sumana was born as the sister of King Pasenadi, one of the great royal devotees of the Buddha. She heard the Buddha preaching a sermon to her brother and she was converted, but she waited a long

time to renounce so she could take care of her grandmother. When her grandmother had died, she was already quite advanced in the stages of the Buddhist religious life because of her practice as a laywoman and to continue that practice, she asked for ordination. The Buddha, knowing her spiritual maturity, spoke this verse to her. At the end of it, she was enlightened. Sumana repeated the verse herself and then she was ordained.

19 Dhamma was born in a respectable family and was married to a suitable husband. She came to trust in the Buddha's teaching and wanted to go forth, but her husband would not allow it. Even so, she devoted herself to practicing what the Buddha taught as a laywoman, living as if she were ordained, including collecting food as alms. One day, she fell down while coming home from collecting alms and she used that mishap as a support for cultivating insight, just like the stick she used to support her body. She was enlightened there and spoke this verse at that time.

20 Dhammapala says that Sangha's story is the same as Dhira's. Pruitt, *The Commentary on the Verses of the Therīs*, 36. This would mean that she also was a concubine in the future Buddha's harem.

21 Sumedha was born the daughter of a king, Koncha, in the city of Mantavati. Her parents arranged a marriage for her with Anikadatta. When she was young, she had gone to the monastery of Buddhist women, together with other princesses and servants. She heard the dhamma from those nuns and began to have faith in the Buddha's teaching. As a young adult, she set her mind on a religious life as a nun. When she overheard her parents arranging her marriage, she became determined to go forth. She had already made considerable progress toward enlightenment before she was allowed to leave her parents' house and once she ordained, she quickly became enlightened.

22 A fuller sense of *pasāditā*, here translated as "converted," would suggest that Sumedha came to feel that she was taken care of, in a profound sense, in this world of suffering and thus she felt at ease; in other words, she discovered that the Buddha taught his teaching for her, no less than for anyone else.

23 That is, even though fools experience for themselves the reality of the four noble truths by experiencing suffering as a result of their desire (which the second noble truth explains as the origin of suffering), they do not see what is being taught as applying to them.

24 The six realms of rebirth in the Buddhist cosmos; the four bad

places of punishment are in hell, and among animals, ghosts, and asuras, the two somewhat better are among humans and gods. Dhammapala makes it clear that it is only rarely and with difficulty that one is reborn among humans or gods. Pruitt, *The Commentary on the Verses of the Therīs,* 355.

25 The Pali verse contains word play on *pabbajjā,* here translated as "going forth." It means both that there is no escape from hell and no chance for Buddhist ordination for those in hell.

26 Buddhas have ten powers in terms of what they can know, ranging from knowing the facts of reality to knowing the past rebirths of all beings and knowing the causal laws of karma that structure the rebirth of beings. Pruitt, *The Commentary on the Verses of the Therīs,* 355.

27 The translation here includes the implication supplied by Dhammapala.

28 There are many difficulties and uncertainties with this verse; for a discussion of possibilities of rectification, see Norman, trans., *The Elders' Verses II Therīgāthā,* 196. The translation here follows Dhammapala. Pruitt, *The Commentary on the Verses of the Therīs,* 357.

29 This verse employs Buddhist technical vocabulary that is used to describe the objective nature of a person: *khanda,* the five aggregates (what makes a person), *dhātu,* the basic elements that make up everything, and *āyatana,* a concept that holds together the internal and external bases of sensory experience, namely, the senses and the objects of the senses.

30 That is, in the six places for rebirth in Buddhist cosmology.

31 The Buddha. See the n. 26 above.

32 The translation is guided by Dhammapala. When the palmyra palm is cut to a stump, it will not send up new shoots, so effectively it is dead. See Norman, trans., *The Elders' Verses II Therīgāthā,* 201; and Pruitt, trans., *The Commentary on the Verses of the Therīs,* 360 for the textual difficulties of the simile.

33 The translation here follows Dhammapala, who in his contextual prologue to the poem of Sumedha says that her parents had decided to give her in marriage to Anikadatta in the city of Varanavati. Pruitt, trans., *The Commentary on the Verses of the Therīs,* 343.

34 The first *jhāna,* that experience, or actually that abolition of experience, that is the result of meditations that withdraw the practi-

tioner from the world, and even from awareness of the self; they are said to be like a turtle withdrawing into its shell.

35 Repeating what her parents had said to her.

36 There is a pun here; it also means "the kingdom has been given up by you."

37 A primeval king who could have any pleasure or object that he wanted in this world.

38 Dhammapala explains that people break the limbs of a tree while trying to get the fruits. Pruitt, trans., *The Commentary on the Verses of the Therīs*, 364.

39 A mountain outside Rajagaha.

40 Dhammapala explains that becoming a "crocodile" represents, metaphorically, gluttony and thus the attractions of returning to lay life. Pruitt, trans., *The Commentary on the Verses of the Therīs*, 369.

41 There is word play here on *amata* as ambrosia and as the deathless, that is, nibbana.

42 One for each of the physical senses.

43 Constructed (*saṅkhataṃ*) objectively, in the sense of made in dependence on other things, and also subjectively, in the sense of being subject to our mental constructions. See also n. 29 above.

44 The translation here follows Dhammapala's gloss, which explains that Sumedha was frightened by a fear of samsara that is the cause of being separated from relatives and other sorrows. Pruitt, trans., *The Commentary on the Verses of the Therīs*, 373.

45 That is, she became enlightened. The six higher powers, or *chaḷabhiññā*, allow one to have direct knowledge of things that otherwise are not known. They are: (1) possessing the divine eye, (2) the divine ear, (3) psychic powers, (4) knowledge of other people's thoughts, (5) recollection of former existences, and (6) knowledge of the destruction of depravities that ooze out from within.

46 A Buddha who lived in an eon previous to the one in which we live.

Selections from Arjuna and the Hunter

1 *Mahābhārata,* critical edition, 3.31.24–42 (*Kairātaparvan*).

2 On Sanskrit *kāvya* poetry, see D. H. H. Ingalls, "Words for Beauty in Classical Sanskrit Poetry," in *Indological Studies in Honor of W. Norman Brown*, ed. Ernest Bender, American Oriental Series 47 (New Haven, Conn.: American Oriental Society, 1962), 87–107.

For a detailed study of Bharavi's *Kirātārjunīya,* see Indira V. Peterson, *Design and Rhetoric in a Sanskrit Court Epic: The Kirātārjunīya of Bhāravi* (Albany: State University of New York Press, 2003). For a brief discussion, see A. K. Warder, *Indian Kāvya Literature,* vol. 3, *The Early Medieval Period: Śūdraka to Viśākhadatta* (Delhi: Motilal Banarsidass, 1977), 198–233.

3   F. Kielhorn, "Aihole Inscription of Pulikesin II. Saka-Samvat 556,"*Epigraphia Indica* 6, no. 1 (January 1900): 1–12.

4   Peterson, *Design and Rhetoric in a Sanskrit Court Epic,* 23–24.

5   Court epic chapters are composed in a variety of meters, with a single meter usually deployed throughout a chapter. The choice of meter is often governed by the topic or mood of the particular chapter.

6   For definitions and descriptions of the Sanskrit court epic, see Peterson, *Design and Rhetoric in a Sanskrit Court Epic,* 7–20; and David Smith, *Ratnākara's Haravijaya: An Introduction to the Sanskrit Court Epic* (Delhi: Oxford University Press, 1985), 1–102; on the major *mahākāvyas,* see Siegfried Lienhard, *A History of Classical Poetry: Sanskrit, Pali-Prakrit.* History of Indian Literature vol. 3, fasc. 1, ed. J. Gonda (Wiesbaden: Otto Harrassowitz, 1984), 159–196.

7   The critic Dandin says that court epics may be based on legend, history, and myth. *Kāvyādarśa* of Daṇḍin, ed. with an original commentary by Rangacharya Raddi Shastri, 2nd ed., K. R. Potdar (Poona: Bhandarkar Oriental Research Institute, 1970), 1.14. The martial metaphor dominates even poems that are not directly about conflict.

8   *Kāvyādarśa* of Daṇḍin, 1.15.

9   *Kāvyādarśa* of Daṇḍin, 1.18. On *rasa,* see Adya Rangacharya, *The Nāṭyaśāstra: English Translation with Critical Notes* (Delhi: Munshiram Manoharlal, 2007), chapters 6 and 7.

10   Bhavari, *Arjuna and the Hunter,* ed. and trans. Indira Viswanathan Peterson, Murty Classical Library of India (Cambridge, Mass: Harvard University Press, 2016), 18.47. Bharavi's preoccupation with these themes, and his polemical style of presenting them in his poem, no doubt stem from the south Indian historical context of his poem. In the first millennium the Deccan region of south India was the site of major contestations between Brahmanical Hinduism and the so-called heterodox religions, Buddhism and

Jainism, which advocated stringent nonviolence and foregrounded monastic practices and ideals.

11 In this chapter Bharavi evokes the *Bhagavadgītā* in many ways: first, by his use of the *śloka* meter, the meter of the two old epics, including the *Bhagavadgītā,* embedded in the *Mahābhārata.* In the *Bhagavadgītā,* Krishna teaches Arjuna, who is reluctant to fight against his cousins and kinsmen in the Mahabharata war, that he must fight. In *Kirātārjunīya* chapter 11, the situation is reversed. Indra tries to tempt Arjuna to give up his weapons and become an ascetic, but Arjuna strongly refuses, citing his duty to gain weapons from gods and fight in the war. In his exhortation to Arjuna to give up his weapons and commit himself to peaceful asceticism (11.10–36) Indra condemns sensual desire and attachment to wealth, using the language of Hindu and Buddhist ascetic texts, which are cast in the *śloka* meter.

12 "Father" is a common form of address for an old man, but here there is an intended irony as well, since Arjuna does not know that this man is in fact his father, Indra.

13 "Kinsmen": A *dāyāda* is literally a lineal kinsman who shares or competes with a person for inheritance rights. The figure of speech is *parikara,* "significant epithets."

14 Mallinatha explains *satyaṃkāra* as an amount of money or other goods paid in advance, either to secure the services of another or to pay in advance, as guarantee, a portion of the amount owed for a service.

15 Both because they cannot bear to do so and because Draupadi has turned away. The courtiers are the sun; Duhshasana the tree; Draupadi, whom he is dragging toward the assembly, the tree's shadow, which turns away from the tree under the gaze of the evening sun but cannot break loose. See *Kirātārjunīya,* 15.33.

16 This idea appears frequently in the *Kirātārjunīya.* See, for example, 11.72–73.

17 "Bright": *śubhra,* literally "white." In Sanskrit literary convention, fame (*yaśas*) is white in color, hence the frequent comparison between fame and the moon.

18 Arjuna refers to the sequence of the four stages of a man's life, the ways of life of a celibate student, householder, forest dweller, and renouncer.

19 The verse resonates with a verse in *Bhagavadgītā* 6.38, where Ar-

juna asks Krishna about the fate of the man who has neither faith nor discipline of action: "Doomed by this double failure, is he not like a cloud split apart (*chinnābhram iva*)?"

Selections from The Life of Harishchandra

1   Hampi was an important Shaiva religious center in the medieval period, alternately spelled as "Hampe."

2   "It haunted me and I must have acted Harishchandra to myself times without number. 'Why should not all be truthful like Harishchandra?' was a question I asked myself day and night. To follow truth and to go through all the ordeals Harishchandra went through was the one ideal it inspired in me. I literally believed in the story of Harishchandra. The thought of it all often made me weep." (Mahatma Gandhi, *Autobiography: The Story of My Experiments with Truth,* New York: Dover Publications, 1983), 23. Sorokin also argues that Gandhi's process of identification with the supreme values of love and truth began at the age of twelve when he chanced on a play about Harishchandra. Pitirim A. Sorokin, *The Ways and Power of Love: Types, Factors and Techniques of Moral Transformation* (Philadelphia: Templeton Foundation Press, 1954), 169.

3   See the discussion by the poet and playwright P. T. Narasimhachar, who recreated the Harishchandra play as *Satyāyana Hariścandra.* P. T. "PuTiNa" Narasimhachar, "Harishchandra on the Path of Truth (Satyayana Harishchandra)," in *A Complete Collection of Musical-Poetic Plays* (Bengaluru: Pu Thi Na Trust, 1998), 774–788.

4   L. A. Suryanarayana, *Raghavanka: Ondu Adhyayana* (Bengaluru: Kannada Sahitya Parishat, 1988); A. N. Krishnarao, "Harishchandra Kavyam," in *Collected Works of A. N. Krishnarao: Literary Criticism,* vol. 4 (Bengaluru: Department of Kannada and Culture, 2011), 147–184.

5   Since most works from the fourteenth to the seventeenth century were written in *ṣaṭpadi* meter, Mugali designates it as the Shatpadi Era. *ṣaṭpadi* was used by such major Kannada poets as Kumaravyasa, Chamarasa, Kanakadasa, and Lakshmisha, which testifies to the influence Raghavanka had on later poets. R. S. Mugali, "Shatpadi," in *Pracheena Kannada Sahitya Roopagalu* (Dharwad: Samaja Pustakalaya, 1997), 183–224.

6   G. S. Shivarudrappa, *Parisheelana* (Mysuru: Usha Sahitya Male, 1967).

7   G. S. Shivarudrappa, *Parisheelana* (Mysuru: Usha Sahitya Male, 1967); Keertinatha Kurtakoti, *Kannada Sahitya Sangati* (Hampi: Kannada Vishvavidyalaya, 1995); G. S. Amur, "Udghatana bhashana," in *Harishchandra Charitra: Samskrutika Mukhamukhi,* ed. Amaresha Nugadoni (Hampi: Kannada Vishvavidyalaya, 2006), 15–27; and Rahamat Tarikere, "Raghavankana kavyatatva: Kelavu tippanigalu," in *Harishchandra Charitra: Samskrutika Mukhamukhi,* ed. Amaresha Nugadoni (Hampi: Kannada Vishvavidyalaya, 2006) 198–212.

8   G. H. Nayaka, "Harishchandra Charitra," in *Harishchandra Charitra: Samskrutika Mukhamukhi,* ed. Amaresha Nugadoni (Hampi: Kannada Vishvavidyalaya, 2006), 219–234; G. S. Shivarudrappa, *Parisheelana* (Mysuru: Usha Sahitya Male, 1967); and G. S. Amur, "Udghatana bhashana," in *Harishchandra Charitra: Samskrutika Mukhamukhi,* ed. Amaresha Nugadoni (Hampi: Kannada Vishvavidyalaya, 2006), 15–27.

9   *Prasāda* are consecrated offerings to god partaken of after worship, in the spirit of a blessing.

10   The descendants of the famous sage Bhṛgu, who had cursed even fire to be all-consuming without letup, were killed by Kritavirya, the son of Vishvavasu.

11   The last and most degenerate of the four world cycles.

12   The status of being a fierce god is conferred on the devotee by Shiva when he takes the devotee in his current, bodily form to Kailasa.

13   An instance in which the different semantic possibilities of the words are exploited for wordplay.

14   Another meaning is "with a lovely bank."

Selections from The Story of Manu

1   The epithet appears in the colophons to each of the chapters and in the patron's address to Peddana in the book's preface: 1.15.

2   In fact, at least two poets before Peddana were called *āndhrakavitāpitāmaha* by their contemporaries: Shivadevayya (thirteenth century) and Koravi Sattenarana (c. 1400).

3   The term is Satayanarayana's, perhaps from a lecture. See Verlcheru Narayana Rao, *Telugulo kavitā viplavāla svarūpam,* 3rd ed. (Chicago: TANA, 2008), 49.

4   Each long cosmic eon, *manvantara,* is presided over by a Manu.

Their stories are told in sequence in the *Mārkaṇḍeyapurāṇa,* from which Peddana has taken the narrative frame for his story of Svarochisha Manu (the sage Jaimini is instructed by Markandeya).

5 Rama of the ax, Parashurama, is a violent avatar of Vishnu. Kubera is the banker of the gods. Shiva appears as Bhikshatana, a naked beggar holding the skull of Brahma in his hand as his begging bowl. Some commentators think the final sentence of the verse refers to a specific tree, *ciguru,* in the Rayalasima area.

6 Bees are said by poets to avoid the champak flowers.

7 The morning prayer to Vishnu is the *vāmanastuti,* a hymn to the god in the first of his human avatars, the dwarf.

8 The *sālagrāma* stone, favored by Vishnu, is free of taint, but Pravara is unwilling even to accept so auspicious and simple a gift from a king.

9 Pravara, as an *āhitâgni* Brahman, maintains the household fire that must never go out.

10 Prayaga, at present-day Allahabad, is the confluence of the Ganga and Yamuna rivers, a pilgrimage site of great importance.

11 Sandal Mountain, Malayachala or Patirachala, is in the far south, in Kerala. Snow Mountain is the Himalaya.

12 Shiva resides at Kedarnath in Uttarancal, the Himalayas; not far to the east is Vishnu's great shrine at Badarinath. The famous Tantric goddess Hingula is located to the far northwest, in Baluchistan in Pakistan.

13 Airavana or Airavata is Indra's elephant mount.

14 The siddha, an accomplished alchemist, can make mercury freeze into a solid *linga.*

15 Bhoja of Dhara was a famed patron of poets including, according to the tradition, the great Kalidasa.

16 Narayana-Vishnu and Nara, the first man, appeared as a closely linked pair at the beginning of time.

17 Bhagiratha worshiped Shiva in order to bring the Ganges down to earth, and indeed the god released the river, which flowed through his matted hair and struck the Himalaya at the site where Pravara is wandering. Agni, god of fire, fell in love with the Krittikas, the wives of the Seven Sages. Here, literally: the three fires (of Vedic offering).

18 The point is that Shiva became a bridegroom, his body smeared in auspicious turmeric. Mena is wife to Mount Himalaya.

19 Literally, yakshas and gandharvas.

Selections from Poems from the Guru Granth Sahib

1   Bards Satta and Balvand depict Guru Nanak passing on his legacy to Angad (see hymns 966–967 of the Guru Granth Sahib [hereafter GGS]). Also Bhai Vir Singh, ed., *Vārāṅ Bhai Gurdas* (Amritsar: Khalsa Samachar, 1977), 1.45.

2   Guru Nanak's life is told in the *Janamsākhīs*. These have come down in a variety of renditions such as the Bala, Miharban, Adi, and Puratan. For a comprehensive study, see W. H. McLeod, *Early Sikh Tradition: A Study of the Janam-sakhis* (Oxford: Clarendon Press, 1980).

3   W. H. McLeod, *Historical Dictionary of Sikhism* (Lanham, Toronto, Oxford: The Scarecrow Press, 2005), 5.

4   The title of Guru Nanak's hymn is derived from *japu,* to recite repetitively. According to *Śabadārath Srī Granth Sāhibjī,* it was called *Japu* "because it was composed to be recited over and over again"—"*jo muṛa muṛa japana laī racī gaī hai.*" *Śabadārath Srī Guru Granth Sāhibjī,* 4 vols. (Amritsar: Shiromani Gurdwara Parbandhak Committee, 1969). Designed for personal contemplation, this inaugural composition of the GGS is not set in the musical framework.

5   "Will," *hukamu,* is the divine order or command.

6   The "written" (*likhiā*) or "writ" (*lekhā*) or "to write" (*likhi*) is an all-embracing Nanakian principle.

7   The original *haumai* is literally "I-me." By constantly centering on the "I," "me," and "mine," the individual is wrenched from their universal root and reduced to a narrow self-centered character.

8   "True by name" is *satu nāmu.* Truth is *the* name of the infinite One, while all other names are merely its aspects.

9   Guru Nanak categorically denounces the theory of incarnation. The One does not descend into the world in any form.

10   Some medieval yoga traditions used sound vibrations as meditational techniques for spiritual liberation, but for Guru Nanak it is the sound of sounds, prior to all sonic distinctions.

11   The Hindu gods of creation (Brahma), preservation (Vishnu), and destruction (Shiva). Gorakhu in the original is Vishnu.

12   A "guru" is not a spiritual master or a goddess or a sacred book as such, but any insight, any awakening to the universal matrix of all beings. Here the term "guru" is not capitalized, except when it refers to the historical Gurus.

13 Stanzas 8–11 bring up the importance of the sonic role in the awakening of the spiritual sensibility. The spiritual achievers are from diverse religious traditions. The siddhas are the eighty-four mystics believed to have attained immortality through the practice of yoga. The *nāthas* trace their lineage to Adinath, the original master, Lord Shiva.

14 The four stanzas on "listening" are followed by four on "embracing" the wondrous name. Like many other Nanakian terms, *manne* is a multivalent term that signifies having trust or faith, remembering, accepting. In my previous works, I translated this term as "remembering." Nikky Guninder Kaur Singh, *The Name of My Beloved: Verses of the Sikh Gurus* (New Delhi: Penguin, 2001), 51, and as "having faith." Nikky Guninder Kaur Singh, *Of Sacred and Secular Desire: An Anthology of Lyrical Writings from the Punjab* (London: I. B. Tauris, 2012), 38, but "embracing" seems more appropriate as it indicates a reaching out to the name and making it a part of the embodied self. Later in stanza 21 Guru Nanak expresses his triple maxim: by listening (*suṇiā*) and by embracing in the mind (*mannia manu*), we evoke love (*kītā bhāu*) for the One.

15 The unspecified "five" (*pañca*) appear frequently in Guru Nanak's compositions. Rather than the "saints" or the "elect," as usually translated, these refer to the five senses, which can be honed into five virtues: truth (*sati*), contentment (*santokhu*), morality (*dharamu*), compassion (*daiā*), and patience (*dhīraju*); or conversely, degenerate into five vices: lust (*kāma*), anger (*krodhu*), greed (*lobhu*), attachment (*mohu*), and pride (*ahaṁkāru*). Guru Nanak also refers to these latter five as "thieves" that rob humans of their authentic self.

16 "Union," *saṁjogu,* with the One.

17 In the original both terms *tanu* and *deha* denote the "body."

18 "Wealth" in the original *ātha* from *artha*. C. Shackle, *A Guru Nanak Glossary* (London: School of Oriental and African Studies, 1981), 24.

19 With slight variation, this passage forms the opening of Asa raga (GGS 347), and also of the evening prayer, which takes its title from the beginning two words of the opening stanza (*so daru,* literally, "that gate," GGS 8). Thus it appears three times in the GGS.

20 Instead of the usual classification scheme of musical modes into ragas and *rāginīs,* their female "consorts," here we have ragas and *parīs,* or "fairies."

21 Dharamraja, the king or judge of *dharamu* (righteousness).

22 Chitra and Gupta are the two attendants of Dharamraja; they record everybody's actions for him.

23 Indra, the king of the gods in Hindu mythology.

24 The four sources of life: egg, fetus, sweat, and earth.

25 Later in this passage it becomes clear that the author is addressing member(s) of the Aipanth; see n. 26.

26 "Mother's sect," Aipanth, one of the twelve sects of yogis who worship Ai Bhavani, a primeval mother goddess.

27 The original *bhaṁḍāraṇi* identifies the treasurer or storekeeper as female.

28 In the original *ikīsa* indicates the single (*ikku*) divine (*isu*), though *ikīsa* is also numeral 21.

29 The five are the five senses. See above n. 15.

30 A metaphor for the good and the bad.

31 Here, as in the preceding stanza, Guru Nanak uses the central pan-Indian term *dharamu,* dharma, denoting religion, virtue, duty, propriety, morality, cosmic order, and law, without the conventional fourfold class division of Indian society (Brahmans, Kshatriyas, Vaishyas, and Shudras). No action is singled out or reserved for anyone. But whatever is done has an effect. The universal injunction plays out: as you sow, so shall you reap.

32 Stanzas 34–37 depict a spiritual journey through the realms of duty (*dharamu*), knowledge (*giānu*), beauty (*saramu*), action (*karamu*), and truth (*sacu*).

33 Dhruva is the polar star.

34 The term *saramu*—designating the third realm in the "Morning Hymn"—is ambiguous. Different translators have derived it from the Sanskrit *śrama,* meaning effort; the Sanskrit *śarman,* meaning joy or bliss; or the Persian *sharm,* meaning shame, humility, surrender. McLeod presents the debate effectively and opts to translate *saramu* as "effort." W. H. McLeod, *Guru Nanak and the Sikh Religion* (Oxford: Clarendon, 1968), 222–223. In the same vein, Talib chooses "spiritual endeavor." G. S. Talib, *Sri Guru Granth Sahib: An English Translation,* 4 vols. (Patiala: Punjabi University, 1984–1990), 21, while Gopal Singh uses the Persian "surrender." Gopal Singh, *Sri Guru Granth Sahib: English Version,* 4 vols. (Chandigarh: World Sikh University Press, 1978), 11. Macauliffe in his notes firmly states, "*Sharm* here is not the Persian *sharm,* shame nor the Sanskrit *sharam,* toil. It is

the Sanskrit *sharman,* happiness." Max Arthur Macauliffe, *The Sikh Religion: Its Gurus, Sacred Writings and Authors,* 6 vols. (Oxford: Oxford University Press, 1963 [1909]), 216. I rely on the "Morning Hymn" own gloss of *saramu* as *rūpu,* "beauty" or "form" (*saramu khaṇḍu kī bāṇī rūpu*—"the realm of *saramu* is beauty itself").

35 "Sharpen" (*ghaṛīai*) means to file a blunt thing like a pencil or a blade.

36 Exegetes and translators have also contested the meaning of *karamu* designating the fourth "Morning Hymn" realm. For a full discussion, see W. H. McLeod, *Guru Nanak and the Sikh Religion* (Oxford: Clarendon, 1968), 223; and N. G. K. Singh, *The Feminine Principle in the Sikh Vision of the Transcendent* (Cambridge: Cambridge University Press, 1993), 86–88. I find "action" an appropriate designation for a realm that is "full of force" and consists of active agents, the "mighty warriors and heroes."

37 Guru Nanak here depicts Sita, the ancient Indian paradigm of female power, in the plural: "*sīto sītā.*" However, translators and exegetes of the "Morning Hymn" have responded differently to Guru Nanak's reference. For further discussion, see N. G. K. Singh, "Translating Sikh Scripture into English," *Sikh Formations* 3, no. 1 (2007): 38–42.

38 The realm of truth is the fifth and final stage of the spiritual journey. The individual comes face to face with infinity itself and partakes of the qualities of the true One.

39 In this final stanza, the fivefold spiritual journey is embodied in the goldsmith artistically designing the sacred word on the crucible of love in his smithy, while vigorously engaged in his everyday social and economic affairs. For an analysis of this passage, see N. G. K. Singh, "Sikh Mysticism and Sensuous Reproductions," in *Ineffability: An Exercise in Comparative Philosophy of Religion,* ed. T. Knepper and L. Kalmanson (Cham, Switzerland: Springer International, 2017), 113–134.

40 The term "awe" I suggest is a better translation of *bhau* than ordinary "fear." Rudolph Otto's familiar phrase *mysterium tremendum et fascinans* perfectly captures Guru Nanak's analogy. In order to produce fresh designs, the goldsmith must ignite the creative fire with the bellows of awe.

41 "Love" in the original is *bhāu* with a long -*ā*-, whereas "awe" (see previous note) is *bhau* with a short -*a*-. The integral relationship

between the emotions of awe (*bhau*) and love (*bhāu*) is constant in Guru Nanak's oeuvre.

42 This concluding lyric (*saloku*) is recited several times during the day by the devout.

Selections from Sur's Ocean

1 Surdas, *Pad Sūrdāsjī kā/The Padas of Surdas,* ed. Gopal Narayan Bahura and Kenneth E. Bryant (Jaipur: Maharaja Sawai Man Singh II Museum, 1982).

2 The 2015 MCLI *Sur's Ocean* edition of Kenneth Bryant does not take account of a considerable group of compositions attributed to Surdas that were recorded within the Dādū Panth. The earliest manuscript included in this group bears the dates 1614–1621 and is to be found in the Sanjay Sharma Sangrahālaya in Jaipur; a total of seven such manuscripts predate 1700. These poems have a strongly *vinaya* orientation. See Biljana Zrnic, "Sūrdās' Poetry Through the Lens of the Community of Dādūpanth," *Asiatische Studien - Etudes Asiatiques* (forthcoming).

3 Kenneth E. Bryant, *Poems to the Child-God: Structures and Strategies in the Poetry of Sūrdās* (Berkeley: University of California Press, 1978), ix–x.

4 Ronald Inden, Jonathan S. Walters, and Daud Ali, *Querying the Medieval: Texts and the History of Practices in South Asia* (New York: Oxford University Press, 2000), 11–12, 48–51.

5 Allison Busch, *Poetry of Kings: The Classical Hindi Literature of Mughal India* (New York: Oxford University Press, 2011), 65–101; compare, Heidi R. M. Pauwels, "Romancing Rādhā: Nāgarīdās' Royal Appropriations of *Bhakti* Themes," *South Asia Research* 25 (2005): 55–78.

6 Double entendre: as nouns, *giri* and *parat* mean not "fall" but "mountain." It is in such a landscape that the ascetic Shiva sits as he shields the earth from the more-than-mountainous weight of the Ganges as she descends from heaven, where she is the Milky Way.

7 Krishna defeated the bull demon Arishta, whose name means evil, calamity, or disaster.

8 Lotus? Pearls? This is the first challenge of many in this puzzle poem. See John Stratton Hawley, *Into Sūr's Ocean: Poetry, Context, and Commentary* (Cambridge, Mass.: Department of South Asian Studies Harvard University, 2016).

9   As Krishna's female manifestation, the flute Murali is compared
     to Mohini, and the liquor of immortality is likened either to the
     overall brilliance of Krishna's face or specifically to the wetness of
     his lips. The waxing and waning moon is a vessel alternately filled
     with and emptied of the translucent divine liquid of immortality,
     called *amṛt* (deathless). Hence when Krishna's face is compared to
     a full moon, it is natural to think of it as endowed with this *amṛt*.
     The *gopīs* protest that Krishna's flute has first access to this moon-
     beam-saliva juice, while they, despite their many efforts to obtain
     him through austere vows, must accept Murali's leftovers trans-
     mitted to them as her music.

10   Perhaps she has in mind the complete absence of concern for
     social conventions that a renunciant adopts, since she speaks of
     having undertaken a purificatory discipline of "mind and words
     and acts."

11   Pleasure, gain, righteousness, and release (*kāma, artha, dharma,
     mokṣa*).

12   The *dān līlā* begins as a morning adventure, but Krishna is so suc-
     cessful in trapping the *gopī* in a quarrel full of "ambrosial words"
     that evening is soon at hand. The poet plays with the opposition
     between night and day by identifying the sun as "the enemy of
     night" (*sārang ripu*). This he contrasts to the moon, whose face is
     marked by shadows that are thought to resemble deer (*mrig cand*).

13   The *gopī* faults Brahma ("the Creator") for not giving her enough
     eyes to take in the sight of Govind, i.e., Krishna.

14   A closely related version of this poem appears under the signature
     of Hit Harivamsh. Rupert Snell, ed. and trans., *The Eighty-Four
     Hymns of Hita Harivaṁśa: An Edition of the Caurāsī Pad* (Delhi:
     Motilal Banarsidass, 1991), 194.

15   Triumph and Victory (*ajay* and *vijay*) are the gatekeepers of Vai-
     kunth, Vishnu's heavenly realm, and are renowned not only for
     this act of eternal cooperation but also for the demonic forms these
     demiurges assume as history develops—this, in response to a curse
     leveled against them by Sanak.

16   When one untangles the intricate knot of references that structure
     this puzzle poem, it comes clear that this is the rainy season. The
     heroine's confidante is admonishing her to abandon her pique and
     accept her lover once again.

17   The confrontation between Arjun and Karna in the Mahabharata

ended in the latter's death and was particularly poignant because the warring protagonists were sons of a common mother, Kunti.

18 Since Radha's beauty is incomparable in "all three worlds" (heaven, atmosphere, and earth), who can this new beauty be? It must be Krishna dressed as a woman; being male, he does challenge Radha's title. In concluding, the *gopī* who speaks urges the two of them to repair to their trysting place, abandoning their "cleverness"—including, presumably, their clothes.

Selections from The Epic of Ram

1 For a more detailed general introduction to the *Mānas* and its author, see Philip Lutgendorf, trans., *The Epic of Ram,* vol 1 (Cambridge, Mass.: Harvard University Press, 2016), vii–xxii.

2 Mohandas K. Gandhi, *An Autobiography, or, The Story of My Experiments with Truth,* trans. Mahadev Desai (Ahmedabad: Navjivan Publishing House, 1968 [1927–1929]), 47; on the role of the *Mānas* in the emerging Hindi literary canon, see Francesca Orsini, "Tulsī Dās as a Classic," in *Classics of Modern South Asian Literature,* ed. Rupert Snell and I. M. P. Raeside, 119–141 (Wiesbaden: Harrassowitz, 1998).

3 According to commentators, this bird, called a *ṭiṭṭibha* or *ṭiṭiharī,* sleeps with its feet in the air out of the false belief that it can thus prevent the sky from falling on it.

4 This list of antique weapons includes several types of spears, as well as several others concerning which commentators disagree as to their precise identity and use.

5 "Gnashing their teeth," *kaṭakaṭāī;* this onomatopoeic verb refers to the chattering sound monkeys, when aroused, make with their bared teeth. In English, however, the chattering of teeth is mainly associated with cold and weakness, hence this translation.

6 "Anguished," *ātura.* Since this word can be both an adjective and a noun (in the latter usage, sometimes meaning "the diseased," "the sick"), some interpret this line to refer to the three classes of Lankan citizens—women, children, and the infirm—who were not conscripted for the battlefield.

7 With this charming giveaway of the battle's outcome, Shiva as narrator reassures his wife not to be alarmed by this apparent setback for Ram's army.

8 "Animosity," *bayara bhāva;* literally, "the emotion of enmity." In

bhakti ideology, any emotional stance that involves concentration on God, including hostility, is considered to yield blessings.

9 In a famous myth, Mandara, the world-axis mountain, was used as a churning rod by the gods and demons to extract the nectar of immortality from the cosmic ocean of milk.

10 "Gaining strength as day waned," *pradoṣa bala pāī;* literally, "gaining the strength of twilight." *Rākṣasas,* whose nature is dominated by the quality of *tamas,* or "darkness," are believed to grow stronger at nightfall.

11 "Dark monsoon clouds and multihued ones of Sharad," *prābiṭa sarada payoda;* the month of Sharad comes at the end of the rainy season, and its more variegated clouds serve as a simile for Ram's simian legions.

12 "Generals," *anipa;* the *Mānaspīyūṣ* treats this word as the name of a third demon, apparently in order to create symmetry with the three substances produced by demonic maya that are mentioned in the next *caupāī.* However, *anipa* means "leader of an army," and Akampan and Atikay are named in other verses as demon generals.

13 "Sharks," *jhaṣa;* both this word and *makara* (the first creature mentioned in this half line) refer to large, carnivorous aquatic creatures, sometimes depicted as crocodiles or fish. For variety, since both appear here, I have used "crocodile" and "shark."

14 In most recensions of the *Vālmīki Rāmāyaṇa,* this character, also known as Malyavan, is identified as Ravan's maternal grand-uncle.

15 Malyavant alludes to well-known mythical exploits of Vishnu, celebrated in the *purāṇas*—the slaying of the demons Madhu and Kaitabh, and of Hiranyaksha ("golden-eyed") and his brother Hiranyakashipu ("gold-clad").

16 "Drew his bow-string to its full extent," *śravana lagi tāne;* literally, "drew it to his ear." This formulaic phrase recurs several times, when a mighty warrior takes aim and prepares to shoot an arrow from his bow.

17 The divine eagle Garuda is the archenemy of snakes and feeds on them.

18 "Male and female goblins," *pisāca pisācī;* Tulsi uses the masculine and feminine forms of a word designating a type of malevolent being, often imagined as an impish fiend.

19 "Nine regions," *nava khaṇḍā;* according to commentators, this refers to traditional subdivisions or "provinces" of the continent of Jambudvipa, an ancient name for the South Asian landmass.

20　"Cremation smoke," *mṛitaka dhūma;* some commentators take this phrase to mean "ashes," and construe the simile as referring to clouds of ash settling on top of glowing embers. Either way, the image is appropriately ominous.

21　"Flame-of-the-forest trees," *kimsuka;* this tree, native to the subcontinent and southeast Asia, produces clusters of bright orange-red blossoms. With its dark foliage, it became a standard poetic trope for the wounded bodies of swarthy heroes.

22　The epithets used for Lakshman in this and succeeding verses, culminating in *dohā* 54—Anant (*ananta* or "endless") and Shesh (*seṣa* or "residual")—are reminders of his identity with the infinite cosmic serpent, known by both of these names, on whom the cosmos and Lord Vishnu rest and who remains when the creation has been dissolved.

23　Some early manuscripts substitute *ananta* for *seṣa* here, a reading preferred by the *Mānaspīyūṣ.* However, it affects neither meter nor meaning.

24　In some myths, at the end of an eon the universe is incinerated by fire emanating from the mouths of Shesh, the thousand-hooded cosmic cobra.

25　Implicit here is the fact that Hanuman, through his devotion, was able to lift and transport the wounded Lakshman, as the demons could not.

26　"Physician," *baida;* the title of a practitioner of Ayurveda, or traditional medicine.

27　The giver of the order is not identified and may be either Sushen or Ram. Other accounts of this episode stipulate that the herb must be administered before sunrise, or the prince will die (and Bharat, too, warns of this at 6.60.3).

28　"Affirming his own might," *bala bhāṣī;* presumably Hanuman does this to assure his distraught master that he will be able to carry out the mission.

29　The Gita Press and *Mānaspīyūṣ* editions offer significantly different readings of this half *caupāī,* based on old manuscript variants. The latter's preferred text (*ahaṃkāra mamatā mada tyāgū*) would be translated, "Renounce your pride, possessiveness, and arrogance."

30　"Pot," *kamaṇḍala;* the water vessel used by ascetics is often made from a dried and hollowed-out gourd, cut so its upper section forms a handle, or it is made out of brass. In oral *kathā,* I have heard it said that Kalnemi's water pot contains poison or a sleeping potion, and when Hanuman rejects the vessel, the demon adopts the alternate strategy of sending him to an enchanted lake containing a hungry female crocodile.

31 "I will initiate you," *dicchā deū.* A ritual bath normally precedes initiation, usually with a mantra. According to some commentators, it is implied that the promised "knowledge" will enable Hanuman to recognize the correct healing herb in the Himalayas (*Mānaspīyūṣ* 6.2.293).

32 According to the *Mānaspīyūṣ* (6.2.294), the sage is not identified in any text, but the *Ānandarāmāyaṇa* states that he cursed the celestial woman for denying him sexual favors, and that he therefore is disgraced and must remain nameless.

33 "Guru gift," *guradachinā;* a gift, in cash or kind, presented to a preceptor after he has performed a ritual, such as initiation with a mantra.

34 In the understanding of devotees, the demon's dying utterance of Ram's name both effects his own salvation and also constitutes the efficacious mantra he had promised Hanuman.

35 "Crown jewel," *tilaka;* though this often connotes an auspicious forehead mark that shows sectarian affiliation, it can also refer to an eminent person or to an ornament for the head.

36 A possible alternative translation is "By your might, master, and keeping the Lord (Ram) in my heart."

37 This extraordinary statement by the paragon of filial piety has occasioned much discussion among commentators. For various interpretations, see *Mānaspīyūṣ* 6.2.309-310.

38 "Blood brother," *sahodara bhrātā;* since this literally means a brother born of the same womb, it technically does not apply to Lakshman, but it suggests Ram's attachment to him as well as his insistence on regarding all three queens as equally his mothers.

39 Once again, this emotional statement is not literally true, since Queen Sumitra gave birth to twins, Lakshman and Shatrughna. Does *eka* ("one" or "sole") imply that Lakshman is her favorite or "primary" son, or the firstborn of the pair? For copious commentary, see *Mānaspīyūṣ* 6.2.315-317.

40 "Heroic mood," *bīra rasa;* "pathos," *karunā;* two of the eight (or nine, in some texts) dominant emotional moods of literature and performance as identified by classical aesthetic theorists.

Selections from The History of Akbar

1 For Jahangir's frank account of this episode, see Nūruddīn Muhammad Jahāngīr Pādishāh, *The Jahangirnama: Memoirs of Jahangir, Emperor of India,* trans. and ed. W. M. Thackston (New York: Oxford University Press, 1999), 32–33.

2 Tamerlane (1336–1405), the progenitor of the Timurid House, to which Akbar and the Mughals of India belonged, was not descended from Genghis Khan, but they had remote legendary ancestors, such as Alanqoa, in common. The Timurids of India were also of Genghisid descent through Babur's mother, Qutlugh-Nigar Khanim, whose father, Yunus Khan, was a direct descendant of Genghis Khan's son Chaghatai.

3 This forms the core of what has been termed *dīn-i ilāhī,* the "divine religion" supposedly propagated by Abu'l-Fazl and a few others of Akbar's coterie. Suffice it to say that no such term is ever used by Abu'l-Fazl himself, nor is any programmatic reinterpretation of religion outlined in the *Akbarnāma*—aside from the constant deprecation of hidebound fundamentalism and the 1579 proclamation of Akbar as *mujtahid* (interpreter of religious law) and *imām* (religious leader) of the age.

Selections from Sufi Lyrics

1 See Lajwanti Rama Krishna, *Panjābī Ṣūfī Poets A.D. 1460–1900* (London: Oxford University Press, 1938), 40–46, and Samina Quraeshi, 2009. *A Journey with the Sufis of the Indus* (Cambridge, Mass.: Peabody Museum Press, 2009), 241–258, which is illustrated with photographs showing the radically modernized appearance of Bullhe Shah's shrine in Kasur today.

2 For recent books of translations that give an excellent idea of the character of this poetry, see Franklin D. Lewis, trans., *Rumi: Swallowing the Sun* (Oxford: Oneworld, 2008), and Paul E. Losensky, and Sunil Sharma, trans., *In the Bazaar of Love: The Selected Poetry of Amīr Khusrau* (New Delhi: Penguin Books India, 2011).

3 For an informed introduction to Sufism, see Carl W. Ernst, *The Shambhala Guide to Sufism* (Boston: Shambhala, 1997).

4 The translations of Qur'anic verses are based on A. Yusuf Ali, trans., *The Holy Qur-an: Text, Translation and Commentary.* 2 vols. (Lahore: Sh. Muhammad Ashraf, 1977).

5 Denis Matringe, "Kṛṣṇaite and Nāth Elements in the Poetry of the

Eighteenth-Century Panjabi Sūfī Poet Bullhe Śāh," In *Devotional Literature in South Asia*, ed. R. S. McGregor (Cambridge: Cambridge University Press, 1992), 190–206. offers a helpful analysis of the Krishnaite and Nath elements in Bullhe Shah's poetry.

6   It has often been observed this famous *kāfī* is modeled on Rumi's great Persian ghazal beginning *cih tadbīr ai musalmānān kih man khud-rā namīdānam, na tarsā nai yahūd-am man na gabr-am nai musalmān-am*, "What can I do, oh Muslims, for I do not know myself. I am not a Christian nor a Jew, not a Zoroastrian nor a Muslim."

7   The Sufi doctrine of "peace toward all" (Persian *ṣulḥ-e kull*) was also adopted in India as a definition of Akbar's policy of religious tolerance toward non-Muslims.

8   "Turk" was a standard term in medieval India for "Muslim," as opposed to Hindu.

9   When Ibrahim, the biblical Abraham, destroyed the idols belonging to his father, Azar, he was sentenced by the evil king Namrud to be burned on a pyre, from which he was rescued by God.

10 Zakariya, the biblical Zechariah, took refuge in a hollow tree from pursuit by the soldiers of the Jewish king Herod. He died when the soldiers sawed through the tree while he was still inside it.

11 Yusuf, the biblical Joseph, was put down a well by his jealous brothers, who sold him into slavery in Egypt; there Zulaikha, the biblical Potiphar's wife, saw him in the slave market and was overwhelmed by love for him.

12 A learned Shaikh who became disgraced through his infatuation with a beautiful Christian girl, for whose sake he had to put on the girdle worn by Christians and to graze pigs. The story comes from the *Mantiq ut Tair* by the Persian Sufi poet Attar.

13 The mysterious twelfth-century Sufi saint Shams misused his miraculous powers to resuscitate the dead son of the king of Ghazna. For this blasphemous claim to possession of God's power over life and death, Shams was sentenced to death by being hanged upside down and flayed alive.

14 The ecstatic saying "I am God" (Ar. *anā 'l-ḥaqq*), literally, "I am the (divine) true reality," proclaiming mystical identity with the divine, is famously associated with the great Sufi martyr Mansur al-Hallaj and led to his execution for blasphemy in Baghdad in 919.

15 The *tilak* is the mark drawn on the forehead as a sign of Hindu religious affiliation, as opposed to the religious practice and duty (*sunnat faraz*) of Islam.

16 The father of the prophet Muhammad.

17 A popular Sufi saying (Arabic *mūtū qabla an tamūtū*) teaches the need to be dead to the world while still living in it.

18 The area near Mathura where Krishna spent his youth as a herdsman.

19 The capital of Ravan's kingdom, attacked by Ram.

20 The letters of the Arabic alphabet often carry important symbolic values, so *alif* is both the first letter of the Arabic alphabet and the first letter of the word "Allah" (الله). The simple shape of *alif,* (ا) A, is identical with the form of the Arabic sign for the number 1 (*aḥad*), which further underlies its use as a Sufi symbol for the divine unity, as opposed to the second letter, *be* (ب), B, which stands for the world of duality.

21 Tegh Bahadur was the ninth Guru of the Sikhs, executed for his faith in Delhi in 1675 by the Mughal emperor Aurangzeb.

22 The biblical Jonah, who was swallowed by a large fish.

23 Ayub, the biblical Job, is always referred to in Bullhe Shah by the epithet "the patient one" (Arabic *ṣābir*). He was tested by God by having his body filled with worms.

24 The Arabic word *al-insān,* "man," indicates the essential unity of God and humanity. It is a shorthand reference to the verse [*wa-laqad khalaqnā*] *al-insān* (Qur'an 15.26), "[And we created] man."

25 The fourteen zones (Arabic *tabaq*) that together make up the entire universe.

26 In the Arabic script, Ahad "the One," i.e., God, is virtually identical with Ahmad, i.e., the prophet Muhammad. Only the letter *mīm* in its very small medial form (*-m-*) marks the difference between *anā aḥad* (انا احد), "I am the One," and *anā aḥmad* (انا احمد), "I am Ahmad, i.e., Muhammad."

27 The Arabic phrase "Let it be, and it was" comes from the end of the verse [*badī'u 'l-samāwāti wa'l-arḍi wa idhā qaḍā amran fa-innamā yaqūlu lahu*] *kun fa-yakūnu* (Qur'an 2.117), "[The creator of the heavens and earth, and when he decrees a thing he but says to it,] 'Let it be,' and it is." It is frequently used by Bullhe Shah to indicate the act of creation.

28 The least elaborate kind of prayer.

29 The refrain expresses the lover's mystical transformation through his experience of the divine self-manifestation, as described in the following verses.

30 Wild geese are symbolically associated with the spiritually aware.

31 There is a deliberately shocking juxtaposition of the pious Muslim formula "In the name of God" (Arabic *bi'smi'llāh*), which is said before undertaking any action, with the Hindu spring festival of Holi. Arabic phrases ending in *'llāh*, "God," recur in the rhymes throughout the poem.

32 From the Islamic profession of faith (P. *kalmā*) *lā ilāha illā 'llāh wa muhammadun rasūlu'llāh*, "There is no god but God, and Muhammad is God's Apostle."

33 A technical term of Sufism (Arabic *fanā fī 'llāh*), used to describe the obliteration of the self in the divine.

34 The scenario of the first day of creation is here developed with the souls of mankind being conceived as girlfriends (*sakhīāñ*). The Arabic word *alast*, "am I not?" begins the verse describing the primal covenant between God and mankind: *alastu [bi-rabbikum] qālū balā shahidnā* (Qur'an 7.172), "Am I not [your lord]? They said, 'Yes, we so testify.'"

35 The phrase "we are nearer" is another scriptural allusion to the immanence of the divine presence in man, from the verse *nahnu aqrab [ilaihi min habli 'l-warīd]* (Qur'an 50.16), "We are nearer [to him than his jugular vein]."

36 An allusion to the favorite Sufi saying *man 'arafa nafsahu [fa-qad 'arafa rabbahu]*, "Whoever has known himself [has known his lord]."

37 The Arabic phrase is from the verse *[fa-ainamā tuwallū] fa-thumma wajhu'llāh* (Qur'an 2.115) "[Wherever you turn,] then there is the face of God."

38 The pious Arabic phrase *sallā 'llāhu ['alaihī]*, which is added to any mention of the Prophet, in modern English Islamic usage often abbreviated as (*pbuh*), i.e., "peace be upon him."

39 The Arabic words are from the verses *fa-'dhkurūnī [adhkurkum] wa-'shkurū lī [wa lā takfurūnī]* (Qur'an 2.152–153) "Then remember me [and I will remember you]. And be grateful to me [and do not be ungrateful toward me]."

40 The Arabic phrase *subhāna 'llāh* is a common exclamation of praise or wonder.

41 The tube (*pickārī*) used to squirt colored dye at other people during the celebration of Holi.

42 The phrase is understood to signify Islam in the verse *sibghatu 'llāhi wa-man ahsanu min allāhi sibghatan* (Qur'an 2.138), "The baptism of God, and who can baptize better than God?"

43 The scriptural phrase *allāhu 'l-ṣamad* (Qur'an 112.2), "God the everlasting one," here daringly indicates the divine presence in man.

44 The countdown to the day of the wedding is calculated by progressively undoing the knots (*gandhīñ*) that have been tied for each day of the waiting period.

45 The overall sense of the poem is powerfully conveyed, but the precise meaning of some verses is not always entirely clear.

46 The word "unstruck" (*anhad*) is usually applied to the mystical sound heard in the yogic process. Here it appears to have the general sense of "imperceptible, invisible."

47 An allusion to the story of Sohni, who went secretly to the river Chenab at night and used an earthenware pot as a float to help her make the dangerous crossing to the far bank, where she would meet her beloved, Mahinval.

48 All editions follow Ruhtaki in printing this *kafi* and the one that follows it as separate poems. Their rhymes *-āriā* and *-oliā* may be different, but these two short poems are otherwise so similar that they are probably variants of a single original that diverged in the oral tradition.

49 This refrain begins with the same words, *kadī ā mil*, as in the previous poem.

50 The Indian cuckoo, regularly cited in poetry for its mournful cry.

51 This half-verse virtually repeats the refrain and appears to be a filler devised to make up the metrical scheme.

52 This remarkable depiction of the strife in contemporary society as a set of disputes between different kinds of snacks and sweets has sometimes been questioned.

53 "Millionaires" (*lakhpati*) are perhaps the name of something to eat, since the other verses begin with the names of sweets.

54 The name of the false prophet whose coming will mark the end of the world and whose teachings will destroy true religion and create social chaos.

55 This represents the actions (Arabic *a'māl*) that are the product of life on earth and upon which the soul will be judged after death.

56 That is, Shah Inayat.

57 See n. 26.

58 This is an abbreviated citation of the divine Tradition (Arabic *ḥadīth qudsī*) addressed by God to the prophet Muhammad: *lau lāka lamā khalaqtu 'l-aflāk*, "If it were not for you [I should not have created] the heavens."

59 The bodily existence (*khākī*) of human beings creates the illusion of separateness between them.
60 The word "Syrian" (*shāmī*), which generates the verse rhyme *-āmī*, is naturally balanced by *rūmī*, here translated as "Turk."
61 The cupbearer (Persian *sāqī*) who in Persian poetry represents the teacher who dispenses the wine of mystical knowledge.
62 Since God is omnipotent, the fault of sin does not lie with man.
63 The Arabic phrase *lā tataḥarraku*, "You do not move [unless I so command]" is a proclamation to man of divine omnipotence. Although it seems to be understood as scriptural, it does not actually occur in the text of the Qur'an.
64 See n. 34. The scriptural quotation reinforces the statements in the preceding verses about the primal compact between God and man, which predates the formal inauguration of Islam.
65 See n. 27.
66 See n. 27.
67 That is, in the world created by God in order that he might be loved.
68 In the Islamic tradition, it was wheat that Adam and Eve were forbidden to eat.
69 The "ignorant one" (*jāhal*) is the prophet Muhammad's arch-enemy, the heathen Abu Jahl. Sabir explains the story: Abu Jahl once hid some stones in his clenched fist and came to ask the Prophet what he had in his hand. Muhammad told him they were stones that would magnify God. Then from his hand could be heard the proclamation, "There is no god but God, and Muhammad is his Apostle." Abu Jahl then fled in discomfiture.
70 See n. 26.
71 God was equally present in the martyr Mansur and in the mullahs standing around to witness his execution.
72 The *Sikandar-nāma* by the Persian poet Nizami describes how the hero, Sikandar, came disguised as an envoy bringing his message to Nushaba, the queen of Azerbaijan, only for her to recognize who he really was.
73 In Jami's Persian poem *Yūsuf Zulaikhā*, Yusuf comes to Zulaikha in her dreams long before the pair actually meet.
74 The magic stone (*pāras*) that alchemically transforms iron into gold.
75 Pharaoh (Arabic *fir'aun*) was the evil ruler of Egypt who persecuted Moses, and who was eventually drowned in the Nile when he tried to pursue him.

76 See n. 27.

77 The phrase "hidden secret" (Persian *sirr-e makhfi*) is a reference to the mystical reason for creation, i.e., that God might be loved.

78 The Arabic phrase comes from a verse describing God's special favoring of mankind: *wa-laqad karramnā* [*banī ādam*] (Qur'an 17.70).

79 To indicate the public announcement either of the glory of Adam's special status in creation or else, according to Muhammad Sharif Sabir, *Bullhe Shāh: Mukammal Kāfiyān* (Lahore: Sayyid Ajmal Husain Memorial Society, 1991), of his disgrace when expelled from paradise.

80 A famous pair of lovers in Islamic romance. The Arab princess Laila was loved so passionately by Qais, who came from a rival tribe, that he was driven mad and became known as Majnun ("the madman").

81 Stains do not show on the blanket worn by a fakir, which is dyed a dark color.

82 The familiar pairing of *alif* and *be* as the first two letters of the Arabic alphabet is here followed by the third letter, *te*, which begins the word *tilāvat*, "recitation of the Qur'an."

83 Later in the alphabet, the letters *sīn* (س) "S" and *shīn* (ش) "SH" are followed by *suād* (ص) "Ṣ," which begins the words *sādak* (Arabic *ṣādiq*), "sincere," and *sābar* (Arabic *ṣābir*), "patient."

84 The comparison of the ring around the neck of a turtledove with the collar around the neck of a slave is a common conceit of Persian poetry.

85 The words *maiñ maiñ*, literally "me, me," are also an onomatopoeic representation of the goat's bleating.

86 There is a play on the literal meaning, "grace," of the name (*ināit*, Arabic *'ināyat*) of Bullhe Shah's master, Shah Inayat.

87 Since God is present in the heart, there is no need to direct appeals to him elsewhere.

88 In this poem, the disguised immanence of the divine is symbolized by the arrival of Ranjha in the dress of a herdsman employed by Hir's father to graze his buffaloes.

89 The alliterative phrase *cākar cāk* ("menial herdsman") emphasizes Ranjha's apparent humble status.

90 That is, since the act of creation, marking the separation of the creator from his creatures.

91 Hir's parents married her off against her will to a man from the Khera tribe, in order to put an end to the disgrace of her relation-

ship with Ranjha. At the end of the wedding ceremony, the Kheras compelled Hir to return with them in a bridal palanquin to her new husband's home.

92 This appears to be the sense of the Panjabi phrase (*mārū kehā jhulāṇā*).

Selections from Selected Ghazals and Other Poems

1 Also see Mir Taqi Mir, *Remembrances,* trans. C. M. Naim, Murty Classical Library of India (Cambridge, Mass.: Harvard University Press, 2019). for further biographical details about Mir. Mir migrated to Lucknow in 1782 and was well received by all accounts, but he remained unhappy with the city. Many verses that he composed in Lucknow over the years reflect a clear sense of loss and loneliness and lack of appropriate patronage.

2 The apple is a common trope for the beloved's chin.

3 "True path": *dīn.* The word more often means "religion," i.e., Islam. My translation maintains the required suggestion of generality.

4 It is apparently the lover's face whose color has faded in disunion. But there are other possibilities, which I have tried to preserve through ambiguity: (1) The lover will make such torrid, stormy love through the night that his color will fade (due to exertion); (2) the beloved's color will fade because of the same exhausting, stormy participation in the lovemaking; (3) the flowers that were fresh last night but have now wilted overnight; (4) it is the color of the night that fades as morning arrives; in other words, the dawn is especially beautiful here at my dwelling.

5 "Hindu" means "Indian."

6 The text is *sadā kar chale,* "called and went away," but *sadā karnā* has also a special meaning: "for the beggar to use the special intonation and words used for begging."

7 In the ghazal world, the counselor is the stock figure of the man of worldly prudence and efficiency; he is always scolding and cajoling the lover, vainly urging him to change his self-destructive ways.

8 The caravan bell is lonely and melancholy because the bell moves on with the caravan but its sound remains behind (a frequent theme in Mir).

9 Black is the color of mourning. Most Arabian tents were black anyway because they were made of felt or leather. But the speaker here implies that Laila's tent was black because they mourned for Majnun in it.

10 The point here is that the rose petal seems bluish when crushed. So do her lips when crushed with kisses.

11 Ghazals in Urdu are written generally with two lines of a verse opposite each other in the same line. The reader customarily put a dot between the two lines of a verse to indicate approval, sometimes with the view of compiling a selection.

12 That is, no stars are visible because of the clouds.

13 It is a common observation that people perspire when they feel ashamed. From here, the transition to "being turned to water with shame" is easy and natural.

14 "Water" in the sense of the brightness of an object, or of a gemstone, as in English, "a jewel of the first water." Some rings or bracelets worn by women had a tiny mirror in place of a gemstone.

15 The word for "beaver" in Urdu and Persian means "water dog."

16 The *bahrī* is a small falcon; there is a delightful pun here on *bahrī* and *baHri*. The latter means "of, or pertaining to, the sea."

17 In Urdu, the word *baHr* is used for both "ocean" and "meter."

18 See n. 14 above.

19 "Wine-duck": a wine goblet in the shape of a duck.

20 This little piece of pornography signals (to those who would take the poem literally) that it's a comic poem.

21 This line and the preceding one are in Persian.

ACKNOWLEDGMENTS

The excerpts in this anthology are selected from bilingual editions published by Harvard University Press's Murty Classical Library of India series. The books from which the selections are chosen were published under the general editorship of Sheldon Pollock.

The following translators' acknowledgments appeared in the original bilingual publications.

Charles Hallisey

This work would not be were it not for Sheldon Pollock. The initial idea that a new translation of the *Therīgāthā* should be done was his; in the long period it took for me actually to do it, he was unflagging in his encouragement, constant in his patience, generous in his guidance and suggestions for improvement, and persistent in his commitment to see it all completed. I thank him for all this and much more is well.

This work would also not be were it not for the generosity, instruction, and example of my teacher, the late G. D. Wijayawardhana, who continues to be for me the very model of what a scholar and a *sahṛdaya* of literature should be.

I am grateful to Beatrice Chrystall for her help with the edition of the Pali text found here. I thank Lilian Handlin for arranging for a copy of the Chatthasangayana edition of the *Therīgāthā* to be sent to me from Burma. I also thank Charles Carstens for his help with some Burmese material and for reading some of the Pali text of the *Therīgāthā* with me, to my benefit.

I am especially grateful to Liyanage Amarakeerthi for his willingness to read with me the work of Martin Wickramasinghe relevant to the appreciation of the *Therīgāthā*. The importance of the work we did together is evident in this introduction and throughout the translation. I am grateful for the encouragement and enthusiasm of Preeti Chopra; her support was crucial for the completion of this work. This work is for my wife, Janet Gyatso. It also would not be were it not for her.

ACKNOWLEDGMENTS

Indira Viswanathan Peterson

I am grateful to the MCLI editorial board and Harvard University Press for inviting me to publish a translation of Bharavi's *Kirātārjunīya* in what promises to be an illustrious series on the Indian classics. It seems especially appropriate to publish Bharavi with Harvard University Press just a little over a hundred years after the first complete translation of the *Kirātārjunīya* in a European language (Carl Cappeller's 1912 German translation) appeared in the Harvard Oriental Series. Working with my editor, Sheldon Pollock, has been sheer pleasure. The translation has benefited in innumerable ways from his careful reading, vast knowledge, friendly and constructive suggestions for improvement, and his unerring taste. I have enjoyed our conversations about translating Bharavi. My debts to Harunaga Isaacson are great. I am deeply grateful to him: for preparing and sharing the Göttingen digital text of the *Kirātārjunīya;* for sending me text editions with various commentaries, including the Munich manuscript of Prakashavarsha's commentary; for alternative readings and new insights into the poem's difficult wordplay chapter; above all, for his friendship and generosity. I thank Dániel Balogh for preparing in record time an accurate *devanāgarī* text for this translation, based on my edition of the text. I am also grateful to Ivy Tillman, Caro Pinto, and Aime DeGrenier of the Mount Holyoke College Library's Research and Technology Support team for helping me prepare the manuscript for submission. Thanks as always to Mark and Maya for their unfailing support.

Vanamala Viswanatha

Given the contemporary state of Kannada culture in which the disconnect with the world of classics is near complete, it is difficult for any one person to undertake the daunting task of translating ancient or medieval Kannada works into English. This translation was a collaborative enterprise to which several scholars and translators generously gave their time, energy, and expertise, always keeping in mind the larger cultural significance of such a project. That said, I am entirely responsible for all choices—big and small—made in the process of translation.

I am deeply indebted to Azim Premji University for supporting this project and giving me time to translate the late N. Basavaradhya, who permitted me to use his edition of the text jointly edited with Pandita S. Basappa; T. V. Venkatachala Shastri, renowned scholar and teacher, for being just a phone call away and clarifying every doubt I raised; Raagu

240

and Niruma, for their touching faith in me and consistent support, which have lit up my work over the decades; K. S. Madhusudana, for his unfailing, rigorous "classes" on making meaning out of Old Kannada texts, his moral and material support through the project, and his help with sourcing published materials on the text; Sheldon Pollock, for his keen editorial eye and open-minded feedback, which made for a better text; David Shulman, for his perceptive reading and fair emendations, which considerably enhanced the quality of this work; Ramdas Rao, who read every word, lending me his well-trained ears and eyes; Sudhi Seshadri, master of compression, for "frenzying" the hunting scenes and for teaching me how to write more concisely; Naresh Keerti, a critical friend, for his enthusiasm for things classical and his passion for Sanskrit translations and Indology; danseuses Chitra Dasharathi and Tulasi Ramachandra for help with interpreting terms in the text related to music and dance; Maitri Vasudev, for making the onerous task of preparing the manuscript joyous with her lively company; and the readers of the translation—T. S. Satyanath, V. B. Tharakeshvar, Du. Saraswathi, Jane Sahi, Janet and Eric Lord, S. N. Sridhar, Rajeshwari Sundar Rajan, C. K. Meena, Krpa, Basavaraja Kalgudi, Dinesh Hassan, and Arshia Sattar—for their comments on the drafts at various stages. Finally, I cannot appreciate enough the daily support and strength offered by my family: Ammu, Aditya, Sharad, and little Aman; Gowru the guru, Padma Chakravarthy and family, and Viswa, who would have celebrated the translation and taken sole credit for it!

Velcheru Narayana Rao and David Shulman
We wish to thank Vadapalli Sesha Talpa Sayee and Kalepu Nagabhushana Rao for their meticulous and efficient production and proofreading of the Telugu text, carried out as a professional courtesy. David Shulman is profoundly grateful to Dr. M. V. Kanakaiah of Rajahmundry for teaching the *Manucaritramu* over the course of seven months and many subsequent shorter visits; the lucidity and precision of his explication of the text are without parallel. Velcheru Narayana Rao taught the text to a particularly congenial group of colleagues and students at the University of Chicago: Gary Tubb, Yigal Bronner, Ilanit Loewy Shacham, Jamal Jones, and Gautham Reddy; their responses were very helpful. For bibliographic help we, as always, are deeply grateful to Parucuri Sreenivas.

Nikky- Guninder Kaur Singh

I am most grateful to Professor Sheldon Pollock for taking me on board, and for including the works of the first Sikh Guru in his visionary project of the Murty Classical Library of India. My special thanks to Professor Archana Venkatesan for reading my manuscript and giving me many excellent suggestions. My thanks to Chief Secretary of the SGPC Sardar Harcharan Singh, Dr. Kulbir Thind, Heather Hughes, and Sharmila Sen for their manifold support, and to my students at Colby College for their engaged conversations. For the profound joy of reading Guru Nanak's poetry, I am grateful to my parents and grandmother, who awoke my interest, and to my brother, who ensures I keep it alive. Thanks too to my resonant drone string, Harry, and to my pick-me-up Bela. But I have no words to thank my editor Francesca Orsini. I dedicate this translation to her. Francesca's inspiration and labor make the impossible possible.

John Stratton Hawley

This translation has been four decades in the making, and we have had a great deal of help along the way. We are both profoundly grateful to Sheldon Pollock—consummate editor at many levels—without whom it would never have reached its final form; and to Monika Horstmann, who evaluated every line of text and translation, lavishing on them the scholarly fruits of a lifetime and the sympathy and good sense of a true connoisseur.

I remember with affection and gratitude the good-humored, supremely intelligent labors of Tom Ridgeway, who transcribed photographs of manuscripts into a digitally accessible form at the University of Washington in the 1980s. Vidyut Aklujkar and Shrivatsa Goswami provided detailed and discerning reviews of Jack's draft translations, resulting in a host of corrections and improvements; Krishna Chaitanya Bhatt and Vimala Mehta started the process as devoted teachers. Mark Juergensmeyer spent countless hours rescuing translations from failure as English verse, and on occasion Linda Hess kindly lent a hand. Many Columbia students have brought Surdas to life in seminars on "Bhakti Texts." Within this group Paul Arney, Amy Bard, Nadine Berardi, Elaine Fisher, Joel Lee, Jim Lochtefeld, Till Luge, Gurinder Singh Mann, Travis Smith, and Hamsa Stainton will see that their insights about specific individual poems have altered the translation for the better. Time and again senior colleagues cheerfully offered their invaluable help. Special thanks go out to Aditya Behl, treasured in memory, and to Allison Busch, Winand Callewaert, Purushottam Goswami, Gurinder Singh Mann, Philip Lutgendorf, Suresh Pandey, Fran Pritchett, Michael Shapiro, and Rupert Snell. Sean Pue, a master of Hindi-Urdu, brought to bear not only that but also his massive expertise on the technical side of things. Vidur Malik, Peter Manuel, Shubha Mudgal, Prem Lata Sharma, and Richard Widdess were generous with their knowledge of music and performance. No one can read a list this long and think that the notion of collective authorship, which we have proposed in relation to Surdas, belongs any more to the past than it does to the present.

Institutions have also played a crucial part. Substantial grants from the National Endowment for the Humanities and the Social Sciences and Humanities Research Council of Canada enabled the *Sūrsāgar* project to be launched in the first place. Supplemental awards from the American Institute of Indian Studies, the John Simon Guggenheim Foundation, the University of British Columbia, the Shastri Indo-Canadian Institute, the University of Washington, Barnard College, and the Leonard Hastings Schoff Fund of the University Seminars at Columbia University have sustained our progress over a very long haul.

Philip Lutgendorf

I am grateful to Rohan Murty for his generosity and to the production staff of Harvard University Press for the extraordinary care and diligence they have brought to the production of this translation series. I thank general editor Sheldon Pollock and coeditor Francesca Orsini for offering me the opportunity to undertake this translation and for their subsequent guidance. I also thank the late Shrinath Mishra, a revered *rāmāyaṇī* (traditional *Mānas* scholar) of Banaras, for his generous help and encouragement, and Pranav Prakash for his careful editing and proofreading of the Devanagari text. Among early mentors who guided me toward this work, I gratefully cite Professors Emeritus Colin P. Masica and the late Kali Charan Bahl of the University of Chicago.

I dedicate this translation to Meher Baba, who inspires me; to the many *Mānas* scholars and devotees who have instructed and encouraged me; and to the memory of three dear mentors and friends—Ramji Pande, A. K. Ramanujan, and Chandradharprasad Narayan Singh ("Bhanuji").

Christopher Shackle

I am most grateful to Leena Mitford and Marina Chellini for helping me with access to materials from the British Library, to Farjad Nabi for his invaluable gifts of books from Lahore, and to Sheldon Pollock both for his original invitation to contribute this volume to the Murty Classical Library of India and for his subsequent steady provision of wise and encouraging editorial guidance.

Shamsur Rahman Faruqi

This book owes much to Sheldon Pollock's meticulous editing. He is the one editor I know who took almost as much pains on editing as I took on the translations. I will always be grateful to him. Thanks are also due to Frances Pritchett, longtime friend and collaborator—she went over the translations at Sheldon's request, and, out of friendly interest, made good suggestions and prepared a most useful glossary.

SOURCES

Abu'l-Fazl: The History of Akbar, Volume 4, Edited and translated by Wheeler M. Thackston (Murty Classical Library of India, Volume 14), Copyright © 2018 by the President and Fellows of Harvard College.

Bharavi: Arjuna and the Hunter, Edited and translated by Indira Viswanathan Peterson (Murty Classical Library of India, Volume 9), Copyright © 2016 by the President and Fellows of Harvard College.

Guru Nanak: Poems from the Guru Granth Sahib, Translated by Nikky-Guninder Kaur Singh (Murty Classical Library of India, Volume 33), Copyright © 2022 by the President and Fellows of Harvard College.

Mir Taqi Mir: Selected Ghazals and Other Poems, Translated by Shamsur Rahman Faruqi (Murty Classical Library of India, Volume 21), Copyright © 2019 by the President and Fellows of Harvard College.

Allasani Peddana: The Story of Manu, Translated by Velcheru Narayana Rao and David Shulman (Murty Classical Library of India, Volume 4), Copyright © 2015 by the President and Fellows of Harvard College.

Raghavanka: The Life of Harishchandra, Translated by Vanamala Vishwanatha (Murty Classical Library of India, Volume 13), Copyright © 2017 by the President and Fellows of Harvard College.

Bullhe Shah: Sufi Lyrics, Edited and translated by Christopher Shackle (Murty Classical Library of India, Volume 1), Copyright © 2015 by the President and Fellows of Harvard College.

Surdas: Sur's Ocean: Poems from the Early Tradition, Edited by Kenneth E. Bryant; Translated by John Stratton Hawley (Murty Classical Library of India, Volume 5), Copyright © 2015 by the President and Fellows of Harvard College.

Therigatha: Poems of the First Buddhist Women, Translated by Charles Hallisey (Murty Classical Library of India, Volume 3), Copyright © 2015 by the President and Fellows of Harvard College.

Tulsidas: The Epic of Ram, Volume 6, Translated by Philip Lutgendorf (Murty Classical Library of India, Volume 31), Copyright © 2022 by the President and Fellows of Harvard College.

A complete list of all Murty Classical Library of India volumes can be found on the series website (murtylibrary.com).